RECEIVING OR REFUSING GOD'S GLORY

A Study of 1 & 2 Kings and 2 Chronicles

Jack W. Hayford
with
Joseph Snider

THOMAS NELSON PUBLISHERS
Nashville

A Study of 1 & 2 Kings and 2 Chronicles
Copyright © 1998 by Jack W. Hayford

Published in Nashville, Tennessee, by Thomas Nelson, Inc.

Printed in the United States of America
1 2 3 4 5 6 7 8 — 03 02 01 00 99 98

CONTENTS

Receiving or Refusing God's Glory (A Study of 1 & 2 Kings and 2 Chronicles) is one of a series of study guides that focus exciting, discovery-geared coverage of Bible book and power themes—all prompting toward dynamic, Holy Spirit-filled living.

About the Executive Editor

JACK W. HAYFORD, noted pastor, teacher, writer, and composer, is the Executive Editor of the complete series, working with the publisher in conceiving and developing each of the books.

Dr. Hayford is Senior Pastor of The Church On The Way, the First Foursquare Church of Van Nuys, California. He and his wife, Anna, have four married children, all of whom are active in either pastoral ministry or vital church life. As General Editor of the *Spirit-Filled Life® Bible*, Pastor Hayford led a four-year project which has resulted in the availability of one of today's most practical and popular study Bibles. He is author of more than twenty books, including *A Passion for Fullness, The Beauty of Spiritual Language, Rebuilding the Real You,* and *Prayer Is Invading the Impossible*. His musical compositions number over four hundred songs, including the widely sung "Majesty."

About the Writer

JOSEPH SNIDER is director of family ministries for Fellowship Missionary Church in Fort Wayne, Indiana. His knowledge of the Bible has been sharpened through experience as a youth evangelist with Young Life in Dallas, a faculty member of Fort Wayne Bible College (now Taylor University, Fort Wayne), and three pastoral positions in Indiana in addition to several years of freelance writing.

Married to Sally Snider, Joe has two grown children, Jenny and Ted. Joe earned a B.A. in English from Cedarville College in Cedarville, Ohio, and a Th.M. in Christian Education from Dallas Theological Seminary.

Of this contributor, the General Editor has remarked: "Joe Snider's strength and stability as a gracious, godly man comes through in his writing. His perceptive and practical way of pointing the way to truth inspires students of God's Word."

THE GIFT
THAT KEEPS ON GIVING

One of the most precious gifts God has given us is His Word, the Bible. Wrapped in the glory and sacrifice of His Son and delivered by the power and ministry of His Spirit, it is a treasured gift—the gift that keeps on giving, because the Giver it reveals is inexhaustible in His love and grace.

Tragically, though, fewer and fewer people are opening this gift and seeking to understand what it's all about and how to use it. They often feel intimidated by it. It requires some assembly, and its instructions are hard to comprehend sometimes. How does the Bible fit together anyway? What does this ancient Book have to say to us who are looking toward the twenty-first century?

Yes. Yes. Without a shred of doubt.

The *Spirit-Filled Life® Bible Discovery Guide* series is designed to help you unwrap, assemble, and enjoy all God has for you in the pages of Scripture. It will focus your time and energy on the books of the Bible, the people and places they describe, and the themes and life applications that flow thick from its pages like honey oozing from a beehive.

So you can get the most out of God's Word, this series has a number of helpful features:

 WORD WEALTH

"WORD WEALTH" provides definitions of key terms.

 BEHIND THE SCENES

"BEHIND THE SCENES" supplies information about cultural practices, doctrinal disputes, business trades, etc.

AT A GLANCE

"AT A GLANCE" features helpful maps and charts.

 BIBLE EXTRA

"BIBLE EXTRA" will guide you to other resources that will enable you to glean more from the Bible's wealth.

 PROBING THE DEPTHS

"PROBING THE DEPTHS" will explain controversial issues raised by particular lessons and cite Bible passages and other sources to help you come to your own conclusions.

 FAITH ALIVE

The "FAITH ALIVE" feature will help you see and apply the Bible to your day-to-day needs.

As you'll see, these guides supply space for you to answer the study and life-application questions and exercises. You may, however, want to record all your answers, or just the overflow from your study or application, in a separate notebook or journal. This would be especially helpful if you think you'll dig into the BIBLE EXTRA features. Because the exercises in this feature are optional and can be expanded as far as you want to take them, we have not allowed writing space for them in this study guide. So you may want to have a notebook or journal handy for recording your discoveries while working through to this feature's riches.

The Bible study method used in this series revolves around four basic steps: observation, interpretation, correlation, and application. Observation answers the question, What does the text say? Interpretation deals with, What does the text mean?—not with what it means to you or me, but what it meant to its original readers. Correlation asks, What light do other Scripture passages shed on this text? And application, the goal of Bible study, poses the question, How should my life change in response to the Holy Spirit's teaching of this text?

If you have used a Bible much before, you know that it comes in a variety of translations and paraphrases. Although you can use any of them with profit as you work through the *Spirit-Filled Life® Bible Discovery Guide* series, when Bible passages or words are cited, you will find they are from the New King James Version of the Bible. Using this translation with this series will make your study easier, but it's certainly not necessary.

The only resources you need to complete and apply these study guides are a heart and mind open to the Holy Spirit, a prayerful attitude, and a pencil and a Bible. Of course, you may draw upon other sources, but these study guides are comprehensive enough to give you all you need to gain a good, basic understanding of the Bible book being covered and how you can apply its themes and counsel to your life.

A word of warning, though. By itself, Bible study will not transform your life. It will not give you power, peace, joy, comfort, hope, and a number of other gifts God longs for you to unwrap and enjoy. Through Bible study, you will grow in your understanding of the Lord, His kingdom and your place in it, but you must be sure to rely on the Holy Spirit to guide your study and your application of the Bible's truths. He, Jesus promised, was sent to teach us "all things" (John 14:26; cf. 1 Cor. 2:13). Bathe your study time in prayer, asking the Spirit of God to illuminate the text, enlighten your mind, humble your will, and comfort your heart. He will never let you down.

My prayer and goal for you is that as you unwrap and begin to explore God's Book for living His way, the Holy Spirit will fill every fiber of your being with the joy and power God longs to give all His children. So read on. Be diligent. Stay open and submissive to Him. You will not be disappointed. He promises you!

The Glory of the Kings
1 Kings 1—16; 2 Chronicles 1—16

His father was David, the man after God's own heart. When still an infant, God Himself gave him a pet name, Jedidiah (2 Sam. 12:24, 25). It meant "Beloved of the Lord." When he grew to manhood, God gave him wisdom. When he used that wisdom to honor God, the Lord also blessed him with staggering wealth and sweeping power. When he neglected that wisdom, he led God's people into staggering sin and sweeping judgment. After him, Israel divided into two kingdoms whose spiritual paths diverged; one seeking the glory, the other shunning it.

Solomon pictured the greater glory of that future Son of David who will sit on the throne of the kingdom of God forever. He also illustrated the glory God extends to all His sons and daughters who submit to His kingdom rule in their lives today and tomorrow, as well as forever. His failure and the failures of his successors warn us not to grieve or quench the glorious Spirit within us.

Lesson 1/Receiving the Glory
1 Kings 1—4;
2 Chronicles 1:1-12
(970–966 B.C.)

In an oriental capital, a wealthy merchant sized up the shrewdness of yet another drifter who had approached him for a job. The old Chinese businessman reached into the pocket of his white jacket and placed a brown rock on the table between himself and the young but shabby European.

"What would you say that is, my fine fellow?" the merchant asked quietly.

A ceiling fan stirred the air slowly somewhere in the darkness above the two men and guttered their candle as the younger one gazed at the shapeless lump on the white cloth.

"I'd say it's an uncut diamond. About five carats," he said, raising his eyes to meet his prospective employer's.

"That's right," the merchant nodded with appreciation. "There isn't a man in ten thousand who can see the worth of such a stone. But cut it, polish it, set it against black velvet in a blaze of light, and its splendor will dazzle everyone."

The wrinkled yellow hand shoved the stone across the table toward the smooth white one. "You recognized it. It's yours. Meet me tomorrow morning at pier six."

God's dazzling glory came to young King Solomon in an equally inauspicious way. He realized divine wisdom was more precious for a monarch than wealth or power. That gift of wisdom, honed and polished through obedience to God's Word, blazed with glory in the world of Solomon's day.

THE KINGDOM IN STEREO

First and Second Kings occupied one ancient Hebrew scroll, as did 1 and 2 Chronicles. When the Old Testament was translated into Greek sometime before the birth of Jesus, the Greek writing took up so much more space than the Hebrew that both Kings and Chronicles required two scrolls and were divided into two books each.

Then the translators of the Greek Old Testament grouped together what we call the Books of Samuel and the Books of Kings and labeled them 1, 2, 3, and 4 Kingdoms. They titled the Books of Chronicles 1 and 2 Remainders because they viewed them as supplemental material to the four Books of Kingdoms.

True, 2 Chronicles does cover the same time span as 1 and 2 Kings, but it's much more than a bunch of leftovers. First and Second Kings showed Israel how to look back and evaluate her kings spiritually; 2 Chronicles urged Israel to look ahead with hope for the house of David and the temple.

First and Second Kings narrate and evaluate the reign of Solomon over the united kingdom of Israel and the reigns of the succeeding twenty kings of the southern kingdom of Judah and the twenty kings of the northern kingdom of Israel. The book spans roughly four centuries.

Record the first, middle, and last major events of the Books of Kings next to their dates.

- 971 B.C. (1 Kin. 1:28–40)

- 722 B.C. (2 Kin. 17:5–18)

- 586 B.C. (2 Kin. 25:1–10)

Although 1 and 2 Kings cover the reigns of forty-one kings of Israel and Judah, only certain key figures receive extensive coverage. They were selected because of their spiritual impact for good or evil. Some key political figures whose spiritual significance was minimal—such as Omri (1 Kin. 16:21–28) and the second Jeroboam (2 Kin. 14:23–29) of Israel—are barely mentioned.

Identify the following kings who "star" in 1 and 2 Kings.

- The world-renowned king of united Israel (1 Kin. 1—11)
- The rebel who founded the northern kingdom and created its trademark calf-worship (1 Kin. 12:12—14:20)
- The king of Israel who epitomized idolatry, greed, and opposition to the prophets of God (1 Kin. 16:29—22:40)
- The king whose bloody reform of Israel fell short (2 Kin. 9—10)
- The reform king of Judah who halted the deadly influence of Ahab's family in the southern kingdom (2 Kin. 11–12)
- The king of Judah who allied with the prophet Isaiah to defeat the Assyrian Empire with prayer (2 Kin. 18—20)
- The king of Judah who valiantly used the Law of God to restore the kingdom spiritually (2 Kin. 22:1—23:30)

In addition to the monarchs of Israel and Judah, 1 and 2 Kings abound with prophets—especially in the northern kingdom—who called the rulers back to obedience to the Lord. Identify the two major prophets of the Books of Kings.

1. (1 Kin. 17—2 Kin. 2)

2. (2 Kin. 19:19—2 Kin. 9:3)

Second Chronicles differs in style from 1 and 2 Kings. Chronicles uses genealogies, lists, and detailed worship instructions to remind a much later generation of Jews that God still had every intention of blessing His people through the line of David and through sincere worship. The writer of 2 Chronicles ignored the apostate kingdom of Israel and focused on the careers of seven godly kings from the line of David. Identify them.

1. The king who built the temple (2 Chr. 1—9)

2. The king who campaigned against idolatry (2 Chr. 14:2—16:14)

3. The king who used a choir for an army (2 Chr. 17:1—21:3)

4. The king who repaired the temple (2 Chr. 22:10—24:27)

5. The godly king who became proud (2 Chr. 26)

6. The king whose reforms focused on the temple (2 Chr. 29—32)

7. The king whose reforms focused on the Law (2 Chr. 34:1—36:1)

SOLOMON'S SECURITY

Turning from an overview of 1 and 2 Kings and 2 Chronicles to the opening chapters of 1 Kings takes you into David's palace in Jerusalem at the end of the aged king's life. David had been thirty years old when he began his forty-year reign over Israel (2 Sam. 5:4). At age seventy he was prematurely enfeebled from the rigors of life on the run from King Saul (1 Sam. 21—31) and the stress of his personal and familial failures (2 Sam. 11—20; 24).

How did David's advisers provide for his growing disability? (1 Kin. 1:1–4)

How did Solomon's half-brother Adonijah prepare to make a claim on the throne of David? (1 Kin. 1:5–10)

Nathan the prophet and Solomon's mother Bathsheba prepared carefully to inform the aged David about Adonijah's plot to replace Solomon as David's successor (1 Kin. 1:11–14). What reasons did each of them give the old king for stirring himself to action?

- Bathsheba (1 Kin. 1:15–21)

- Nathan (1 Kin. 1:22–27)

When informed of the rebellion against his wishes, David showed himself capable of more decisiveness and action than Adonijah, Joab, and Abiathar may have expected. How did King David go about guaranteeing Solomon's succession to the throne? (1 Kin. 1:28–40)

 BEHIND THE SCENES

Both Adonijah and Solomon made their claims to the throne of Israel at springs just outside Jerusalem. En Rogel (1 Kin 1:9) was just beyond the juncture of the Kidron and Hinnom valleys south of the capital. Gihon sprang from the slopes of the Kidron Valley just outside the eastern city wall. En Rogel was only about a kilometer from Gihon.

When Abiathar's son Jonathan brought the rebels news of Solomon's accession to the throne, he focused on David's role in everything. What did he say David had done to make Solomon king? (1 Kin. 1:41–48)

How did the rebels react to Jonathan's news? (1 Kin. 1:49, 50)

Nathan and Bathsheba had expected Adonijah to execute Solomon if he succeeded in seizing the throne (1 Kin. 1:21). How did Solomon respond to Adonijah's failed coup? (1 Kin. 1:51–53)

 KINGDOM EXTRA

Humility refuses to promote or exalt itself, trusting the Lord to bring advancement. It quickly acknowledges the Lord when anything it does is recognized, knowing that all accomplishments are realized through God.

Avoid self-promotion. Rely upon the Lord to bring promotion to you. Remember: He who exalts himself will be humbled (Matt. 23:12).[1]

Until David died—whether a few weeks or several months later—he and Solomon ruled Israel as co-regents. When death neared, David gave Solomon final counsel about spiritual necessities and internal security issues. What did David consider spiritually essential to be a godly king? (1 Kin. 2:1–4)

What did David advise about three individuals he felt he had to keep an eye on at all times?
• The unpredictable and ambitious general Joab (1 Kin. 2:5, 6)

• The descendants of his faithful supporter Barzillai (1 Kin. 2:7)

- The old agitator for the rights of King Saul's descendants to be king (1 Kin. 2:8, 9)

After David's death (1 Kin. 2:10–12), Solomon had to deal with three unpleasant internal security issues. Two of them involved people David had warned him about and the other involved a second attempt by Adonijah to move back into the royal limelight.

What concerns prompted Solomon to order the execution of his older half-brother Adonijah? (1 Kin. 2:13–25; see 2 Sam. 3:7; 12:8; 16:21)

When Solomon forced Abiathar, the priest who had supported Adonijah's rebellion, into retirement at his home in Anathoth (1 Kin. 2:26, 27), Joab realized that his days were numbered. How did Solomon reason that Joab had to be executed, even though he sought sanctuary at the altar? (1 Kin. 2:28–35)

Solomon confined Shimei to Jerusalem so he could not conspire with pro-Saul forces in Benjamin (1 Kin. 2:36–38). How did Shimei's behavior three years later demonstrate that he was a threat to Solomon? (1 Kin. 2:39–46)

 FAITH ALIVE

How can your loyalty to new spiritual leaders help establish them securely in the tasks God has for them?

Do you think the way Solomon inherited problems from David's reign illustrates that every leadership transition will

face problems, or do you think Solomon's situation was
unusual? Why do you think so?

SOLOMON'S WISDOM

After Solomon handled the problem people left over from
David's reign, he enjoyed unusual peace and prosperity. He
became strong because the hand of the Lord was on him,
blessing him at every turn (1 Kin. 2:46; 2 Chr. 1:1). Egyptian
pharaohs did not marry their daughters to foreigners as a way
of cementing international alliances. But the pharaoh at the
time of Solomon's reign broke precedent because he could see
that something of great international significance was happen-
ing in Israel.

BEHIND THE SCENES

During the time of the Book of Judges, Israel adopted
the pagan custom of offering sacrifices on high places (ele-
vated hilltops). Since many of these high places were old
Baal sites, this practice was expressly forbidden to the
Israelites (Lev. 17:3, 4). But in certain exceptions the Lord
gave His approval for His people to worship Him at a high
place (1 Sam. 9:12–14). Since the tabernacle of Moses and
the bronze altar were at the great high place at Gibeon (1
Chr. 16:39; 21:29; 2 Chr. 1:3–6), Solomon's sacrifice there
was not seen as idolatrous. The high places were not finally
done away with until the reign of Josiah (2 Kin. 23:8).[2]

Why do you think the Lord gave Solomon the opportu-
nity to ask of Him whatever he wished? (1 Kin. 3:3–5)

What was so admirable about Solomon's request for wisdom? (1 Kin. 3:6–12)

Why do you think the Lord chose to bless Solomon with all the things he hadn't asked for in addition to the wisdom he did request? (1 Kin. 3:13–15)

 KINGDOM EXTRA

God is the only source of true wisdom, and He promises to give it to anyone who asks for it. Wisdom begins with the fear of the Lord and finds its fulfillment in the love of others.

Do not presume to know how to do what the Lord has called you to do. Cleave to the Lord. Depend upon Him for wisdom. Choose to believe that God will give wisdom to all who ask for it (see James 1:5).[3]

Using the following topics, show how Solomon's handling of two prostitutes, each claiming to be the mother of the same baby, illustrated the quality of the wisdom God had given him. (1 Kin. 3:16–28)

• Wisdom in focusing an endlessly circular argument.

• Wisdom in getting to the heart of the issue.

• Wisdom in discovering the truth.

Why do you think the Holy Spirit selected a small, personal matter rather than a big, political incident as the primary illustration of the quality of Solomon's wisdom?

First Kings 4 begins with a summary of the wise organization Solomon implemented in his kingdom. He created a cabinet of officials who oversaw various aspects of his government (vv. 1–6). He divided Israel (minus Judah) into twelve tax districts under governors to support the monarchy on a rotating basis for a month each year (vv. 7–19).

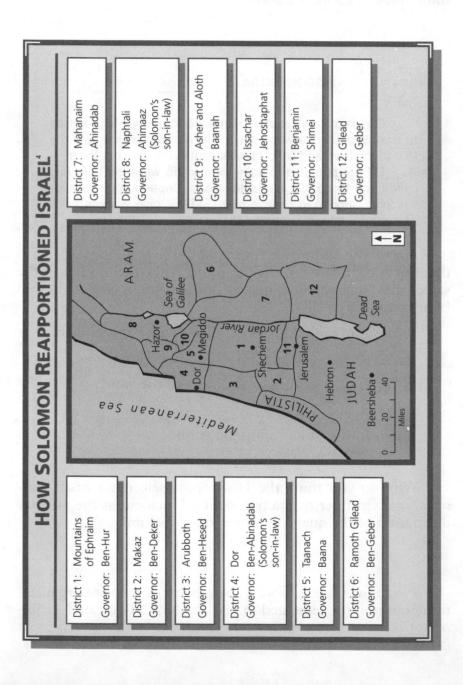

HOW SOLOMON REAPPORTIONED ISRAEL[4]

District 1: Mountains of Ephraim
Governor: Ben-Hur

District 2: Makaz
Governor: Ben-Deker

District 3: Arubboth
Governor: Ben-Hesed

District 4: Dor
Governor: Ben-Abinadab (Solomon's son-in-law)

District 5: Taanach
Governor: Baana

District 6: Ramoth Gilead
Governor: Ben-Geber

District 7: Mahanaim
Governor: Ahinadab

District 8: Naphtali
Governor: Ahimaaz (Solomon's son-in-law)

District 9: Asher and Aloth
Governor: Baanah

District 10: Issachar
Governor: Jehoshaphat

District 11: Benjamin
Governor: Shimei

District 12: Gilead
Governor: Geber

King Saul's monarchy had been small and simple. David's had become large and more complicated. Solomon's became highly structured and efficient. Why is wisdom so vital to keep a large nation united and happy in times of peace and prosperity?

 FAITH ALIVE

In what kinds of situations have you been prompted by need and by the Holy Spirit to ask God for wisdom? (James 1:5)

How has God responded in help to your prayers for divine wisdom?

SOLOMON'S GLORY

The greatness of Solomon's kingdom was the culmination of a long spiritual process. God had blessed King David with many military victories and greatly expanded territory because David had been a man after God's own heart (1 Sam. 13:14). David had wanted to build a temple for the Lord, but God refused to permit it because he had been a warrior rather than a man of peace (1 Chr. 22:8). Solomon, whose name meant "Peace," would take all of David's accomplishments to the next level, the level of glory.

Describe the glories of King Solomon's reign in each of these categories. (1 Kin. 4:20–29)

• The extent of his domain

• The plenty of his provisions

- The security of his subjects

- The organization of his administration

Describe the wisdom of King Solomon as it expressed itself in each of these areas. (1 Kin. 4:29–34)

- In comparison with other wise men

- In its subject matter

- In its effect on those who heard of it

 WORD WEALTH

Glory in the Old Testament has the idea of "weightiness," "dignity," and "substance." The noun originally meant "heaviness," and came to denote honor and authority. "Lightness" represented vanity, instability, and emptiness. God's **glory**—His honor, renown, and majesty—culminated in His visible splendor, which filled Solomon's temple and will someday fill all the earth (1 Kin. 8:11; Num. 14:21).

In the New Testament, **glory** translates a noun that originally referred to an opinion or estimation someone was held in. By extension the word meant "reputation" or "esteem." New Testament writers uniformly attached the idea of God's **glory** to His splendor, radiance, and majesty.[5] Such glory is inherent in God's character. He chose to share a portion of His glory with Solomon by blessing him with wisdom, wealth, and might.

KINGDOM EXTRA

No text in the Bible more magnificently declares God's sovereign power than 1 Chronicles 29:10–16. There is no one like the Lord, the almighty One, whose glory fills the universe. And yet, in the center of this grand anthem of acknowledgment to that towering truth, David asserts that although the kingdom is God's (v. 11), God gives resources that are man's to administer. Verse 14 literally reads, "Everything that exists is from You, and we administer it from Your hand." God is the fountainhead of all life and power; man is the appointed heir for its management.[6] Solomon experienced the glory of representing God as His administrator more than any other Old Testament king.

 FAITH ALIVE

How have you seen the glory of God displayed through the work of the Holy Spirit in your church and in your own life?

God expressed His glory through the wisdom He gave King Solomon. Through what parts of your personality and spiritual giftedness do you imagine God wants to show His glory?

1. *Spirit-Filled Life® Bible* (Nashville: Thomas Nelson Publishers, 1991), 525, "Truth-in-Action through 1 Kings."

2. Ibid., 490, note on 1 Kings 3:2–4.

3. Ibid., 525, "Truth-in-Action through 1 Kings."

4. *The Word in Life Study Bible* (Nashville: Thomas Nelson Publishers, 1996), 595, Map of "How Solomon Reapportioned Israel."

5. *Hayford's Bible Handbook* (Nashville: Thomas Nelson Publishers, 1995), 617, "Glory."

6. Ibid., 669, "The Kingdom of God."

Lesson 2/The Flowering of Glory

1 Kings 5—8;
2 Chronicles 2:1—7:10
(966—946 B.C.)

When asked the secret of his success, J. Paul Getty reportedly said, "Rise early, work late, and strike oil!"

But few of us have any prospects of striking oil. Our search for success is more like that of the reader who called Information to find the telephone number for *Theatre Arts* magazine. "I'm sorry," the operator drawled after a lengthy pause, "but there is no one listed by the name of Theodore Arts.

"It's not a person," the caller explained. "It's a publication. I want *Theatre Arts.*"

The operator's voice grew cold, and she spoke in clear, loud tones: "I told you, we have no listing for Theodore Arts."

The caller's temper flared and he shouted, "Listen, you ninny. The word is Theatre: T-H-E-A-T-R-E."

The operator's training helped her control herself, and she replied sweetly and finally, "Sir, that is not the way to spell Theodore."

When King Solomon's success flowered into its fullest glory, it wasn't because he stumbled onto sudden wealth. It wasn't because he broke through a mass of petty obstacles holding him back. Solomon's glory flowered because his eyes were fixed fully on the Lord and His service. Everything else fell into place around worshiping God.

Solomon's Temple

Before King David died, he had yearned to build a temple for the Lord, but God told David that his son would fulfill his dream (1 Chr. 28:6). The Holy Spirit gave David the plans for the temple (vv. 11, 12), and David devoted much of his energy during his final years to storing wealth and collecting material for it (29:2–5). He shared his passion with his son Solomon and encouraged him to make the temple of the Lord his chief objective when he became king (28:20).

What occasion struck King Solomon as an opportune time to begin the temple project? (1 Kin. 5:1)

What preparations had Solomon made in advance of this occasion? (2 Chr. 2:1, 2, 17, 18)

What requests did Solomon make of Hiram, king of Tyre? (1 Kin. 5:2–6; 2 Chr. 2:3–10)

How did Hiram, king of Tyre, respond to Solomon's requests for assistance in building the temple of the Lord? (1 Kin. 5:7–9; 2 Chr. 2:11–16)

What were the terms of the treaty Hiram and Solomon made with one another? (1 Kin. 5:10–12)

How did these segments of Solomon's temple labor force operate? (1 Kin. 5:13–18)

- The 30,000 Israelite conscripts

- The 150,000 alien slave laborers

- The supervisors

- The skilled laborers from Tyre

BEHIND THE SCENES

Tyre was the chief city of the Phoenician civilization that controlled most of the seafaring commerce of the Mediterranean Sea. Tyre exported timbers from the Lebanon mountains to places as distant as Babylon and Egypt. The coastal region controlled by Tyre was too rugged to support much agriculture, so the Phoenicians regularly imported foodstuffs from Israel and other agricultural peoples. Solomon's treaty provided for a one-time payment to the Phoenician workers (2 Chr. 2:10) and annual payments to King Hiram (1 Kin.

JERUSALEM: DAVID'S CITY[1]

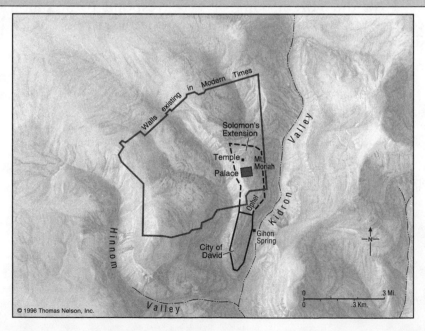

© 1996 Thomas Nelson, Inc.

5:11) that went on for twenty years (9:10). These put a heavy burden of taxation on Israel that contributed to social unrest later (see 12:4).

When did Solomon begin to build the temple of the Lord? (1 Kin. 6:1; 2 Chr. 3:2)

Where did Solomon build the temple of the Lord? (2 Chr. 3:1)

Describe the basic structure of the temple Solomon built for the Lord. (1 Kin. 6:2–10)

Describe the interior decoration of Solomon's temple. (1 Kin. 6:14–35; 2 Chr. 3:5–14)

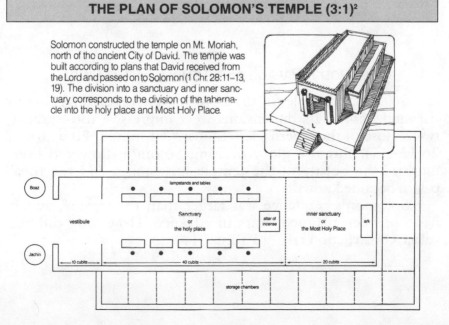

THE PLAN OF SOLOMON'S TEMPLE (3:1)[2]

Solomon constructed the temple on Mt. Moriah, north of the ancient City of David. The temple was built according to plans that David received from the Lord and passed on to Solomon (1 Chr. 28:11–13, 19). The division into a sanctuary and inner sanctuary corresponds to the division of the tabernacle into the holy place and Most Holy Place.

Boaz

lampstands and tables

vestibule

Sanctuary
or
the holy place

altar of
incense

inner sanctuary
or
the Most Holy Place

ark

Jachin

10 cubits — 40 cubits — 20 cubits

storage chambers

How long did it take Solomon to construct the temple of the Lord? (1 Kin. 6:37, 38)

 FAITH ALIVE

When Solomon built the temple of the Lord, he employed the best builders in the world, the best structural materials, the costliest, finest decorations, and tons of gold. Nothing else he would ever do approached the temple in quality.

What would you like to be your greatest accomplishment for the Lord?

What have you done to prepare for it?

How are you making sure that He gets your very best?

SOLOMON'S PALACE AND TEMPLE FURNISHINGS

Solomon's temple for the Lord was impressive in its materials and design. Its dimensions were impressive too—exactly twice those of the tabernacle (compare 1 Kin. 6:2, 20 with Ex. 26:15–25). But the glory of King Solomon flowered even more as the beauty of the temple furnishings and the royal palace became known.

Solomon's residence was larger than the temple, and it had not been planned years in advance. How long did the palace construction take? (1 Kin. 7:1)

BEHIND THE SCENES

The royal palace consisted of the House of the Forest of Lebanon (1 Kin. 7:2), the Hall of Pillars (v. 6), the Hall of Judgment (v. 7), his own personal residence (v. 8), and a residence for Pharaoh's daughter (v. 8). According to the Jewish historian Josephus, these were not separate buildings, but sections of a single palace.[3]

Describe each of these components of the palace complex.

* House of the Forest of Lebanon (1 Kin. 7:2–5, 9–11)

* Hall of Pillars (1 Kin. 7:6, 9–11)

* Hall of Judgment (1 Kin. 7:7, 9–11)

* Personal quarters (1 Kin. 7:8, 9–11)

* Pharaoh's daughter's personal quarters (1 Kin. 7:8–11)

BEHIND THE SCENES

Solomon built the temple of the Lord north of David's Jerusalem on the ridge known as Mount Moriah. A thousand years earlier Abraham had offered Isaac to the Lord there (Gen. 22:2). King David had bought the hilltop when he saw the angel of the Lord there at the time of a plague (1 Chr. 21:14, 15, 25, 26; 2 Chr. 3:1).

Solomon built his palace complex adjacent to the temple area, and the walls of Jerusalem were extended to encompass this northern addition. The temple sat in the middle of a raised courtyard in which the priests ministered (1 Kin. 6:36; Jer. 36:10). Around that was a second courtyard where worshipers gathered to observe and participate in the priest's services (2 Kin. 23:12). A final wall encompassed the palace complex and temple area within a "great court" that pictured the connection between the Lord and "the throne of David" (7:12).

Who did the Lord provide to ensure the beauty of the temple, and what were his areas of expertise? (1 Kin. 7:13, 14; 2 Chr. 2:13, 14)

Describe the most ambitious of Huram's temple decorations. (1 Kin. 7:15–22; 2 Chr. 3:15–17) (The difference in heights mentioned in these two passages probably reflects an ancient copyist's confusion of similar numerical symbols.)

Describe the temple's altar of sacrifice. (2 Chr. 4:1)

Describe the temple's central source of water for purification. (1 Kin. 7:23–26; 2 Chr. 4:2–5)

Describe the temple's facilities for distributing water for purification to different areas of the grounds. (1 Kin. 7:27–39; 2 Chr. 4:6)

 BEHIND THE SCENES

The bronze casting method Huram used to make many of the temple articles depended on the clay found between Succoth and Zaretan (1 Kin. 7:46). A clay form was made in the shape of the center of a hollow pillar or the inside of the great sea. Then a layer of wax was applied to the clay core to the proper thickness and sculpted to the contours and designs of the final object. Special clay overlaid the wax. The whole was slowly baked to harden the clay. The wax was withdrawn through vents, and molten bronze injected through the same openings. Large objects were very difficult to make this way, highlighting Huram's skill.[4]

Describe the gold work Huram prepared for the temple of the Lord. (1 Kin. 7:48–59; 2 Chr. 4:7, 8, 19–22)

What was the final step Solomon took in honor of his father to finish the temple of the Lord? (1 Kin. 7:51; 2 Chr. 5:1)

 FAITH ALIVE

What serve as the most prominent reminders in your life (like the pillars in Solomon's temple) that you are totally dependent on the Lord? If you need to designate some reminders of your dependence on Him, what will they be?

In what areas of your Christian experience do you devote the most effort and skill to live for the Lord with the kind of excellence Huram gave to his temple work?

THE LORD ENTERS THE TEMPLE

Solomon completed temple construction in the eighth month of the eleventh year of his reign (1 Kin. 6:38). He did not bring the ark to the temple and dedicate it until the seventh month of the following year (8:2). The furnishings may have been crafted in those eleven months. Perhaps details of staffing and supplying the temple had to be made. One thing is certain. King Solomon wanted to dedicate the temple at the time of the Day of Atonement and the Feast of Booths, Israel's great times of repentance and remembrance of deliverance from Egypt.

How did Solomon celebrate bringing the ark of the covenant from the tent where David had housed it (2 Sam. 6:17) to the temple? (1 Kin. 8:1–5; 2 Chr. 5:2–6)

Describe how the ark of the covenant was placed in the Most Holy Place of the temple. (1 Kin. 8:6–8; 2 Chr. 5:7–9)

 BEHIND THE SCENES

Moses placed a golden pot filled with manna (Ex. 16:33, 34) and Aaron's rod which budded (Num. 17:10) in the ark of the covenant (Heb. 9:4) along with the stone tablets on which God wrote the ten commandments (Ex. 40:20) with His finger. By the time of Solomon, the pot of manna and Aaron's rod were lost or stolen in military raids (1 Kin. 8:9; 2 Chr. 5:10).

How did the presence of the Lord manifest itself when the priests placed the ark of the covenant in the Most Holy Place of the temple? (1 Kin. 8:10, 11; 2 Chr. 5:11–13)

 KINGDOM EXTRA

The service of the priests and Levites as they installed the ark in the temple (2 Chr. 5:11–13) demonstrates the power in unity of praise, thanksgiving, and music: (1) the trumpeters and singers *were as one;* (2) to make *one sound* in praise and thanksgiving to the Lord, saying, "For He is good, for His mercy endures [lasts] forever"; (3) the house (temple) was filled with a cloud (the glory of God's presence).

Remember, even in praise, thanksgiving, and worship, "God is not the author of confusion" (1 Cor. 14:33). Anything said or done that draws attention to the praiser/worshiper and away from God, Jesus, and the Holy Spirit needs to be reconsidered.[5]

 BIBLE EXTRA

Solomon asserted that the Lord had indicated before that He would make His dwelling in the dark cloud. Look up the following passages that connect God's presence with a dark cloud and summarize the incident.

- Exodus 14:19–25

- Exodus 19:16–20; 24:15–18

- Exodus 40:34–38

- Isaiah 6:3, 4

- Mark 9:2–7

What role did Solomon say each of these played in establishing the temple of the Lord? (1 Kin. 8:14–21; 2 Chr. 3–11)

- The Lord

- David

- Solomon

FAITH ALIVE

In what circumstances of life have you glimpsed the glory of God? How has that changed your understanding of who God is?

Since Christians as individuals (1 Cor. 6:19, 20) and congregations (3:16) are today temples of the Holy Spirit, what can we do to stay aware of His glorious presence within ourselves and our church bodies?

SOLOMON DEDICATES THE TEMPLE

Probably the high point of Solomon's fabled career as king of Israel was when the glory of the Lord filled the temple, and he knelt on a bronze platform (2 Chr. 6:13) before the assembled nation and poured out his soul in praise to the living God. This dedicatory prayer reveals the depth of Solomon's insight into God's character and His desire to respond to the earnest, honest prayers of His people in all of the situations of life.

Look up these verses and trace the changes in Solomon's posture through the course of his dedicatory prayer and blessing of the congregation of Israel. (1 Kin. 8:22; 2 Chr. 6:12, 13; 1 Kin. 8:54, 55)

What things did Solomon affirm about God as the basis of his prayer? (1 Kin. 8:22–27; 2 Chr. 6:12–18)

What was the gist of Solomon's lengthy prayer? (1 Kin. 8:28–30; 2 Chr. 6:19–21)

Identify the seven situations in which Solomon asked God to heed prayers directed toward the temple.

1. (1 Kin. 8:31, 32; 2 Chr. 6:22, 23)

2. (1 Kin. 8:33, 34; 2 Chr. 6:24, 25)

 KINGDOM EXTRA

In Solomon's prayer of dedication, he points to the importance of confessing the Lord's name (2 Chr. 6:24). *Yadah,* the Hebrew word for "confess," is derived from *yad,* meaning "an open or extended hand." Just as a closed fist represents rebellion, an open hand indicates peace, submitted service, or surrender. Solomon approached God (2 Chr. 6:12) with open, extended hands, in a worship-filled confessing of God's faithfulness with thanksgiving and praise. Such a stance will never be loveless or arrogant, and neither earth nor hell can successfully protest this confession of faith in heaven's power.[6]

3. (1 Kin. 8:35, 36; 2 Chr. 6:26, 27)

4. (1 Kin. 8:37–40; 2 Chr. 6:28–31)

5. (1 Kin. 8:41–43; 2 Chr. 6:32, 33)

6. (1 Kin. 8:44, 45; 2 Chr. 6:34, 35)

7. (1 Kin. 8:46–53; 2 Chr. 6:36–39)

Solomon quoted Psalm 132:8–10 as a final connection between his temple dedication and his father David's movement of the ark into Jerusalem many years earlier (see 2 Sam. 6). What important requests did Solomon make by means of this quotation? (2 Chr. 6:41, 42)

In his final words to the people, what did Solomon express about the faithfulness of the Lord and the faithfulness of Israel? (1 Kin. 8:56–61)

What happened after Solomon's dedicatory prayer to confirm the Lord's positive response to it? (2 Chr. 7:1–3)

How did Solomon and Israel expand the national festival of the Feast of Booths and use it to celebrate the dedication of the temple? (1 Kin. 8:62–66; 2 Chr. 7:4–10)

 FAITH ALIVE

Think back through the last month or two and list all the different circumstances in which you turned to the Lord in prayer.

In what sense is God high above everything involving us as people, and in what sense has He intimately involved Himself in the tiniest details of our lives?

What spiritual blessings have you gained from praising the Lord aloud in the presence of other believers who support you and echo your praise?

1. *Spirit-Filled Life® Bible* (Nashville: Thomas Nelson Publishers, 1991), 448, map—"Jerusalem: David's City."
2. Ibid., 615, "The Plan of Solomon's Temple."
3. Ibid., 495, note on 1 Kin. 7:1–8.
4. Ibid., 77.
5. Ibid., 617, "Kingdom Dynamics, 2 Chr. 5:13, Power in Unity of Praise."
6. Ibid., 619, "Kingdom Dynamics, 2 Chr. 6:24–31, The Meaning of 'Faith's Confession.'"

Lesson 3/The Weight of Glory

1 Kings 9—11; 2 Chronicles 1:13–17; 7:11—9:31 (946—930 B.C.)

George Herman Ruth broke into major league baseball in 1914 with the Boston Red Sox as an overpowering left-handed pitcher. He also could hit home runs—rare occurrences in those days, when the ball stayed in the infield most of the time. So the Red Sox played "the Babe" in the outfield when he wasn't pitching to keep his bat in the game.

The owner of the Red Sox needed money to finance a Broadway show he was backing, so he sold Babe Ruth to the New York Yankees in 1920, and the rest is baseball history. New York City embraced Babe Ruth as a hero and celebrated every mighty blow off the bat of "the Sultan of Swat." Attendance soared and Yankee Stadium was built in the Bronx and dubbed "the house that Ruth built." In 1927 he hit sixty home runs. In his career he belted 714. Both marks were thought untouchable until Roger Maris broke the first in 1961 and Henry Aaron the second in 1974.

George Herman Ruth had been born to poverty in Baltimore in 1895. He grew up in his father's saloon and defied all parental authority. His mother and father declared him incorrigible and turned him over to an orphanage where he learned two things: a craft and baseball.

George Herman Ruth went from the orphanage to baseball superstardom with nothing in between. He had no concept of self-discipline. He ate hot dogs by the dozens to the amusement of his teammates. He drank like a fish. He womanized without restraint. Everyone looked the other way because of his prodigious talents on the field.

The Yankees let Babe Ruth go in 1934. He wanted to manage, but no one took him seriously. He had never managed himself, conventional wisdom ran. He could never manage a team. The pressures of fame overwhelmed Babe Ruth the man. No one knows how much those pressures dimmed the blazing talents of Babe Ruth the athlete.

SOLOMON UNDER OBLIGATION

God gave King Solomon gifts of wisdom and leadership that made him the Babe Ruth of Israel's kings. His inauguration and his early reign were nothing short of spectacular. The surrounding nations scrutinized and tested Solomon's wisdom again and again, both to admire it and to look for flaws that could be exploited. The weight of glory was great on the young king. Unlike Babe Ruth, Solomon had been thoroughly prepared by his father, King David, and by the Lord. How well would he bear the weight of glory?

How had the Lord shown His positive response to King Solomon's dedication of the temple at the time it occurred? (2 Chr. 7:1, 2)

How did the Lord show His approval of Solomon's work thirteen years after the temple was completed? (1 Kin. 9:1–3; 2 Chr. 7:11, 12)

Solomon began building in the fourth year of his reign (1 Kin. 6:1). He spent twenty years building the temple and his palace (9:10). Solomon was in the twenty-fourth year of his forty-year reign (11:42) when the Lord appeared to him the second time (9:2). What did the Lord want Solomon to have firmly in mind as he entered the final portion of his reign? (1 Kin. 9:4–9; 2 Chr. 7:13–22)

The Lord was renewing the Davidic covenant with Solomon (see 2 Sam 7:12–16). He had emphasized the unconditional elements of the covenant to David, but to Solomon He stressed the conditions to be met if the blessings of the covenant were to be enjoyed. How do you think Solomon must have reacted to the prospect of his vast realm and precious temple being in ruins because of royal disobedience? (1 Kin. 9:7–9; 2 Chr. 7:20–22)

 KINGDOM EXTRA

Second Chronicles 7:14 is the best-known and most-beloved verse in Chronicles. This verse, perhaps more than any other single verse in all Scripture, sets forth the stipulations for Israel to experience God's blessing. It had special significance to the first readers of 2 Chronicles because they had actually experienced the truth of the principle God had spoken to Solomon.[1] It's still true that humility and prayerful seeking after God are prerequisites of national spiritual renewal and healing.

In addition to his covenant obligation to obey God, Solomon had a twenty-year history of treaty obligations to Hiram, king of Tyre (1 Kin. 9:10, 11). What did Solomon and Hiram trade for Solomon's future building projects? (1 Kin. 9:11, 14)

How did Hiram react to Solomon's collateral? (1 Kin. 9:12, 13)

What did Solomon do when Hiram returned his collateral for the loan of 120 talents (about four tons) of gold? (2 Chr. 8:2)

What building projects (in addition to the temple and the palace) did King Solomon use the gold he got from Hiram to complete? (1 Kin. 9:15–19; 2 Chr. 8:2–6)

SOLOMON'S EMPIRE[2]

EUPHRATES RIVER

Tiphsah

Possible limit of northern border, along the Euphrates River (1 Kin. 4:24).

PHOENICIA

THE GREAT SEA

Tadmor

Hiram of Tyre furnished materials and craftsmen to build the temple and royal palace in Jerusalem (1 Kin. 5).

Tyre

Hazor

Megiddo

Important defense outposts included the cities of Tadmor, Hazor, Megiddo, Beth Horon, Gezer, and Baalath (1 Kin. 9:15–19).

Gezer Beth Horon
Baalath Jerusalem

Gaza   DEAD SEA

Thousands of laborers built the temple and Solomon's royal palace at Jerusalem (1 Kin. 5—7).

RIVER OF EGYPT

Ezion Geber

Possible limit of southern border, in the vicinity of Gaza along the northern border of Egypt (1 Kin. 4:21, 24).

Shipping fleet on the Red Sea for trade with nations to the south (1 Kin. 9:26–28).

RED SEA

BEHIND THE SCENES

The old City of David topped the ridge known as Zion. Solomon's temple and palace crowned the ridge called Moriah. The Millo (1 Kin. 9:15) indicates the fill work and system of supporting terraces that created a saddle between Zion and Moriah on whose various levels houses and buildings were constructed. At various times in Jerusalem's history, the terraces of the Millo would need to be shored up and strengthened (see 2 Chr. 32:5). Solomon's wall extensions (1 Kin. 9:15) encompassed the Millo and the temple-palace area.

What was Solomon's sole military campaign in his forty-year rule? (2 Chr. 8:3, 4)

Why do you think Solomon felt he had to build defensive fortresses throughout his realm and maintain a standing army with horses and chariots? (1 Kin. 9:19; 2 Chr. 8:6)

What royal obligation fulfilled by Solomon is reported in each of the following passages:

- 1 Kings 9:20, 21; 2 Chronicles 8:7, 8

- 1 Kings 9:22, 23; 2 Chronicles 8:9, 10

- 1 Kings 9:24; 2 Chronicles 8:11

- 1 Kings 9:25; 2 Chronicles 8:12–15

- 1 Kings 9:26–28; 2 Chronicles 8:17, 18

Solomon's responsibilities and his wealth seemed at times to be as vast as his wisdom. The pressures to go his own way had to be immense. In addition to the will of God, what other guiding principle did Solomon follow? (1 Kin. 9:1, 19; 2 Chr. 7:11) What risks did this introduce in Solomon's life?

 FAITH ALIVE

In the space below, list four primary areas of obligation in your life and explain how you try to keep those under the direction of God's will rather than the impulses of your passions and changing ideas.

1.

2.

3.

4.

SOLOMON IN THE PUBLIC EYE

As the kingdom of Israel pressed against Egypt to the southwest and the Mesopotamian powers to the northeast, King Solomon was noticed by the political leaders of his day. As his commercial fleet sailed to more distant ports of call, King Solomon grabbed the attention of the economic leaders of the time. As his writings became known, King Solomon claimed the ears of the intellectual leaders of his age.

Why did the queen of Sheba come to see King Solomon? (1 Kin. 10:1; 2 Chr. 9:1a)

Why do you imagine she came to Jerusalem with such an impressive retinue? (1 Kin. 10:2; 2 Chr. 9:1b)

What things about Solomon and his court left the queen of Sheba breathless? (1 Kin. 10:3–5; 2 Chr. 9:2–4)

What things had the queen of Sheba observed about Solomon that she considered important enough to report to him? (1 Kin. 10:6–9; 2 Chr. 9:5–8)

What was the wealth of Solomon like, and how did it affect the way he reacted to the generous gifts of the queen of Sheba? (1 Kin. 10:10–13; 2 Chr. 9:9–12)

 BEHIND THE SCENES

Sheba probably was the kingdom of the Sabeans on the southwestern tip of the Arabian peninsula, occupying the area presently known as Yemen. It is the only watered portion of the peninsula. Its agriculture was good, and the deserts to the north protected it from attack. Sheba controlled the commercial sea lanes between Africa, India, and the Near East and was very prosperous. Probably Solomon's new commercial fleet attracted the attention of the queen.

Solomon's income of gold was nearly twenty-five tons each year (1 Kin. 10:14). How did his wealth make King Solomon conspicuous in each of these areas?

• Palace ornamentation (1 Kin. 10:16, 17; 2 Chr. 9:15, 16)

• The throne (1 Kin. 10:18–20; 2 Chr. 9:17–19)

- Abundance of gold (1 Kin. 10:21–23; 2 Chr. 9:20–22)

What characteristic of Solomon's wisdom was obvious to everyone? (1 Kin. 10:24; 2 Chr. 9:23)

How did Solomon's interaction with people from all around the ancient Near East increase his wealth, prestige, and power? (1 Kin. 10:25–29; 2 Chr. 9:24–28)

 BEHIND THE SCENES

Archaeology suggests the chariot cities of Solomon were Hazor, Megiddo, and Gezer (1 Kin. 9:15). Chariots were of little use in the hills of central Palestine, but those three cities guarded approaches to the highlands from neighboring plains where horses and chariots would be effective. Israel had not used horses and chariotry before, but Solomon developed both to the point that he became a favorite middleman in the sale of both throughout the region.

 FAITH ALIVE

What advantages does a Christian have in witnessing for Christ if he or she is in the public eye?

What are the disadvantages in living for Christ of being a very public figure?

What special help from God's Spirit do well-known Christian men and women need to be successful as representatives of the Lord?

How can you pray for your pastor or other prominent Christians you know to support them under the scrutiny of public attention?

SOLOMON SUCCUMBS TO PRESSURE

In Deuteronomy 17:16, 17, God said that kings of Israel should not accumulate horses, wives, or wealth. Solomon amassed all three, but he is faulted in the pages of Scripture only for the second one—marrying many foreign wives. In Deuteronomy, the ban on horses involved becoming dependent on Egypt. Israel would do that at later points in her history, but not during Solomon's reign. His incredible wealth was a gift from God (1 Kin. 3:13). However, Solomon stumbled badly when he gave his heart completely to pagan women.

Solomon probably married women from the royal families of the surrounding nations as part of treaties with their fathers. What response of Solomon to these pagan women made him vulnerable to them? (1 Kin. 11:1, 2)

What was the predicted and actual result of Solomon's entanglement with pagan wives? (1 Kin. 11:2–4)

Throughout 1 and 2 Kings the writer evaluates monarchs by how they compared to David. Solomon becomes the first of many to be compared unfavorably to David, whose heart stayed true to the Lord even though he sinned grievously at times. How did Solomon reveal that his heart had strayed from true devotion to the Lord? (1 Kin. 11:4–8)

BEHIND THE SCENES

The gods and goddesses Solomon worshiped as favors to his wives represented the decadence of Canaanite culture that had provoked God's holy war against it in the days of Joshua. Ashtoreth was the Canaanite goddess of fertility whose worship involved not only sexual rites, but astrology. The worship of Milcom or Molech included human sacrifices, especially of children. The worship of Chemosh was equally cruel and also centered in astrology.[3]

The writer of 2 Chronicles omitted the account of Solomon's forays into idolatry to please his many pagan wives. The chronicler wrote for people keenly aware of the consequences of spiritual apostasy to assure them of God's continued love and blessing. While the chronicler focused exclusively on Solomon's successes, the writer of 1 Kings warned much earlier readers of future dangers. What did the Lord tell Solomon would be the result of his apostasy? (1 Kin. 11:9–13)

In the last years of Solomon's rule, after his heart had cooled toward the Lord and become inflamed toward idols, God allowed adversaries to trouble Solomon's kingdom. The first adversary appeared on the southern edge of Israel. He had been harboring a grudge since the days of David. Who was he, what was his complaint against Solomon, and what was his goal? (1 Kin. 11:14–22)

What backing did this adversary have that must have puzzled Solomon? (1 Kin. 11:18–22)

A second adversary emerged on the northern edge of Israel. Who was this adversary and how did he trouble Solomon and Israel? (1 Kin. 11:23–25)

This adversary became a major problem late in Solomon's reign, but he had been active much longer. How long had he led rebellious forces against Solomon? (1 Kin. 11:25)

The most serious adversary who arose to trouble Solomon late in his reign came from inside Israel. Solomon had instituted the use of forced labor by Israelite men on public works projects. The temple, the palace, the expansion of Jerusalem, the fortification of chariot cities, and other projects continually took Israelite men from their fields one month out of three (1 Kin. 5:14). Heavy taxes and forced labor became the causes of social unrest in Israel. Describe the man who would later lead a revolt against these oppressive policies. (1 Kin. 11:26–28)

What did a prophet from the former worship center of Shiloh have to tell Jeroboam about his future? How did he tell him? (1 Kin. 11:29–33)

How did the Lord explain to Jeroboam through the prophet why He was leaving one tribe under the control of the descendants of David? (1 Kin. 11:34–36)

What remarkable promises did the Lord make to Jeroboam and his descendants? (1 Kin. 11:37–39)

How did King Solomon respond when he discovered what the Lord had told Jeroboam through Ahijah the prophet? Did Solomon act more like King David or King Saul in this response? (1 Kin. 11:40)

FAITH ALIVE

What entanglements with the world do you feel most susceptible to?

What would be the spiritual consequences of succumbing to those entanglements as completely as Solomon gave in to idolatry?

How do you think we can recognize when difficulties in life are God's chastening for sins of which we need to repent?

How do you think we can remain like David throughout life without fading toward the end in our commitment to the Lord?

1. *Spirit-Filled Life® Bible* (Nashville: Thomas Nelson Publishers, 1991), 620, note on 2 Chr. 7:14.

2. *Nelson's Complete Book of Bible Maps and Charts* (Nashville: Thomas Nelson Publishers, 1993), 112, "Solomon's Empire."

3. *Spirit-Filled Life® Bible*, 503, note on 1 Kin. 11:5–7.

Lesson 4/Neglecting the Glory
1 Kings 12—16;
2 Chronicles 10—16
(930—868 B.C.)

In the motion picture *Charade,* Audrey Hepburn and Cary Grant search for a treasure hidden in plain view by Hepburn's mysterious husband who was murdered by former partners in crime. Everyone—good guys and bad guys—looks desperately for a clue to something of great value among the few personal effects Charles left on the train from which he was thrown.

It takes a child casually pursuing his hobby to discover by chance that the stamps on an unmailed letter are the three rarest specimens in the world. Every villain and hero in the story had handled the envelope and glanced at the stamps without once recognizing their glory. Once the value of the stamps was known, black hearts wanted to grasp them for selfish ends. Only good hearts appreciated their beauty and wanted to see them put in their proper place.

The Lord chose David and his descendants to rule His people, and He chose Jerusalem as the place where His name would dwell in the temple Solomon built. After the time of Solomon, not many rulers appreciated the glory God had designed into the Davidic monarchy and His worship at the temple. Civil war divided Israel, and many kings looked no further than their own power and glory. They used religion to promote their own ends. Special indeed were the ones who treasured the glory of God's kingdom and His praise.

POLITICAL AND SPIRITUAL FOLLY

Solomon's son Rehoboam didn't seem to regard becoming king of Israel as a major accomplishment. If he had paid attention to the honor and obligation associated with ruling the people of God and protecting the temple of God, he might have fared differently. As it was, he made mistake after mistake and inadvertently fulfilled the prophecy of Abijah the Shilonite (1 Kin. 11:29–40).

After Rehoboam succeeded his father Solomon as king in Jerusalem, he went to Shechem in the territory of Ephraim to be confirmed as king of the northern tribes as well (1 Kin. 12:1; 2 Chr. 10:1). What happened to disturb Rehoboam's coronation at Shechem? (1 Kin. 12:2–4; 2 Chr. 10:2–4)

Rehoboam asked for a three-day period in which to formulate a response to the request of the northern tribes of Israel (1 Kin. 12:5; 2 Chr. 10:5). How did Rehoboam reach the conclusion that he did? (1 Kin. 12:6–11; 2 Chr. 10:6–11)

KINGDOM EXTRA

God's leaders serve Him on the people's behalf, not vice versa. Leaders, be wise and seek counsel from other seasoned and fruitful leaders. Avoid the exclusive counsel of untried leaders who have borne little fruit.[1]

What happened when Rehoboam refused to consider the grievance of the northern tribes of Israel? (1 Kin. 11:12–16; 2 Chr. 10:12–16)

How did the ten northern tribes of Israel formalize their break with Judah and its ally Benjamin who remained loyal to Rehoboam? (1 Kin. 12:17–20; 2 Chr. 10:17–19)

What was Rehoboam's immediate response to the rebellion of the northern tribes of Israel? (1 Kin. 12:21; 2 Chr. 11:1)

A KINGDOM DIVIDED[2]

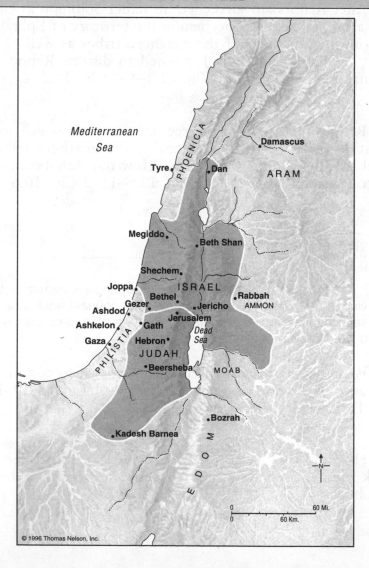

Mediterranean
Sea

Damascus

Tyre Dan   ARAM

PHOENICIA

Megiddo
Beth Shan

Shechem

Joppa   ISRAEL
Bethel   Rabbah
Gezer   Jericho   AMMON
Ashdod
Ashkelon   Gath   Jerusalem
Gaza   Hebron   Dead
PHILISTIA   Sea
JUDAH
Beersheba   MOAB

Bozrah

Kadesh Barnea

EDOM

N

0   60 Mi.
0   60 Km.

© 1996 Thomas Nelson, Inc.

How did the Lord react to Israel's rebellion and Rehoboam's preparations for war? (1 Kin. 12:22–24; 2 Chr. 11:2–4)

After Israel crowned Jeroboam king, he built up Shechem as his capital and fortified Penuel as an outpost east of the Jordan (1 Kin. 12:25). What was the biggest concern Jeroboam had about the stability of his throne? (1 Kin. 12:26, 27)

What does this concern reveal about Jeroboam's confidence in the prophetic word of the Lord which promised him an enduring dynasty dependent only on his family's obedience to the law of God? (1 Kin. 11:37, 38)

How did Jeroboam counterfeit each of the following to protect his control over the northern tribes of Israel?

• The Lord God (1 Kin. 12:28)

• The temple (1 Kin. 12:29–31)

• The priesthood (1 Kin. 12:31, 32; 13:33)

• The annual festivals (1 Kin. 12:32, 33)

What was God's assessment of Jeroboam's alternative gods, holy places, priests, and festival? (1 Kin. 12:30; 13:34)

What prophetic warning did the Lord send to Jeroboam while he worshiped at Bethel? (1 Kin. 13:1–3)

[icon] WORD WEALTH

Sign translates a Hebrew noun that denotes a miracle, sign, or wonder. It occurs thirty-six times in the Old Testament, first in Exodus 4:21 where God mentions the "wonders" Moses would perform before Pharaoh. This term adds to the notion of the miraculous an element of illustration or example of a spiritual truth.[3] In this reference, the splitting of the altar demonstrated the accuracy of the further prophecies of the man of God.

What confirmation did the Lord give to King Jeroboam that His warning was a true prophecy? (1 Kin. 13:4–6)

How had the Lord underlined for His prophet the seriousness of his holy mission into spiritually corrupted territory? (1 Kin. 13:7–10)

Why do you imagine the old prophet living at Bethel lied to his brother prophet and induced him to disobey the Lord? (1 Kin. 13:11–18)

What would the death of the deceived prophet have taught the people of Israel about the dangers of listening to lying spiritual leaders? (1 Kin. 13:23–25)

How do you think the old prophet felt when the Spirit of God compelled him to speak the truth to the younger prophet to whom he had lied? (1 Kin. 13:19–22, 27–32)

How was Jeroboam's sin worse after he ignored the prophetic word and example of the Lord than before? (1 Kin. 13:32–34)

FAITH ALIVE

In what areas of your life are you tempted to protect yourself by worldly means (as Jeroboam did with his idols) rather than trust the Lord to fulfill His promises?

How do you think you could tell when a friend was being less demanding of you than the Lord and inadvertently tempting you to compromise (as the old prophet did to the man of God)?

ABANDONED BY GOD

Solomon's son Rehoboam may have demonstrated arrogance as he assumed the throne of David in Jerusalem, but Jeroboam demonstrated indifference to the prophetic word of God and the spiritual future of Israel when he began to rule the northern tribes from Shechem. He immediately abandoned the Lord who had given him the opportunity to become a great and righteous king. After warning him sternly (1 Kin. 13:1–10), the Lord shortly began to punish the apostate king of the northern tribes.

Jeroboam's son who became ill (1 Kin. 14:1) was not a small boy. His name Abijah meant "The Lord Is My Father," indicating a time of birth when Jeroboam was still devoted to the living God. He was old enough to have a reputation for spiritual goodness (v. 13). Why do you think Jeroboam did not seek a word from one of the prophets in Israel, perhaps the old prophet in Bethel (see 1 Kin. 13)?

Why did Jeroboam particularly want to hear a prophetic word from Ahijah the Shilonite? What kind of message do you imagine he expected from Ahijah? (1 Kin. 14:2)

The gift King Jeroboam sent with his disguised wife was a poor person's gift of the best farm products. What do you think Jeroboam wanted to accomplish by deceiving Ahijah about the identity of who was petitioning him? (1 Kin. 14:2–4)

What should King Jeroboam have realized when he heard that the blind prophet was waiting for his wife to identify her and reveal the fate of his son? (1 Kin. 14:5, 6, 12, 13)

What did the prophet who had given Jeroboam good news before tell him as the direct sequel to that first prophecy? (1 Kin. 14:7–11)

How did God further spell out the effects of King Jeroboam's sin of making idolatry official in the northern tribes of Israel?

- Immediate consequences for Jeroboam (1 Kin. 14:14)

- Long-range consequences for the northern kingdom of Israel (1 Kin. 14:15, 16)

 BEHIND THE SCENES

Ahijah's prophecy about Jeroboam's son came true as soon as Jeroboam's wife entered the gates of Tirzah (1 Kin. 14:17). By the end of Jeroboam's twenty-two-year reign he had already moved his capital city from Shechem (12:25) to Tirzah, some seven or eight miles further north in the hill country of Ephraim. Jeroboam was having trouble getting established. The search for a satisfactory seat of government in Israel was far from over.

Write an obituary for King Jeroboam based on 1 Kings 11:26—14:20.

 FAITH ALIVE

Who has God used in the past or present to point out sin in your life and call you to repentance?

On the following scale circle the number that best rates your responsiveness to confrontation about sin.

1	2	3	4	5	6	7	8	9	10
TOTAL DENIAL		GRUDGING ADMISSION		EMBARRASS- MENT		SIMPLE CONFESSION		DEEP SORROW	

Why does trying to conceal our sin make it worse when it finally becomes known?

PROTECTED BY GOD

While King Jeroboam of Israel found himself at odds with the Lord, the early kings of Judah found themselves the objects of God's grace as descendants of King David. They didn't all respond to that grace, but their kingdom benefited from the goodness of the Lord. Notice that the author of 1 Kings gives short, evaluative summaries of the faithfulness of these kings, while the chronicler devotes much more space to God's gracious initiatives toward them.

How do the authors of 1 Kings and 2 Chronicles characterize the overall course of Rehoboam's reign? (1 Kin. 14:22–24; 2 Chr. 12:14)

The chronicler reported that Rehoboam quickly fortified a chain of defensive outposts along the western, southern, and eastern borders of Judah (2 Chr. 11:5–12), but left the northern frontier with Israel open. What happened because he left that border open? (2 Chr. 11:13–17)

After the three years of godly influence from the influx of Levites and priests from the northern tribes (2 Chr. 11:17), Rehoboam began to forsake the Lord and lead Judah after him (12:1). What was the punishment for Rehoboam's departure from the Lord? (1 Kin. 14:25; 2 Chr. 12:2–4)

How did the Lord deal with Rehoboam to humble him at his time of great danger? (1 Kin. 14:26–28; 2 Chr. 12:5–12)

After listing the sources they relied on for information about Rehoboam (1 Kin. 14:29; 2 Chr. 12:15), Kings and Chronicles note his death, burial, and succession by his son, Abijam (1 Kin. 14:31) or Abijah (2 Chr. 12:16). It's likely that the former was his personal name and the latter his crown name.[4] First Kings mentions ongoing war between Jeroboam and Abijam/Abijah (15:7). Second Chronicles reports a very important battle between Abijah and Jeroboam (13:3). How did Abijah explain the state of hostilities to his northern opponents? (2 Chr. 13:4–12)

What was the outcome of this battle between the 800,000 troops of Jeroboam and the 400,000 troops of Abijah? (2 Chr. 13:13–20)

When Abijam/Abijah died after his three-year reign (1 Kin. 15:8; 2 Chr. 14:1), his son Asa succeeded him as king of Judah. King Jeroboam of Israel still had two years left to rule (compare 1 Kin. 14:20 and 15:9). Jeroboam overlapped three kings of Judah. Asa was beginning a forty-one year reign

(1 Kin. 15:10) that would span seven kings of Israel. How did the writer of 1 Kings characterize the entire reign of Asa? (1 Kin. 15:11)

In the first peaceful decade of Asa's reign (2 Chr. 14:1) he engaged in his first round of reforms. How did King Asa strengthen the kingdom of Judah? (2 Chr. 14:3–8)

When Judah was invaded by a massive army of Egyptian mercenaries, how did King Asa defeat them? (2 Chr. 14:9–15)

How did the Lord motivate King Asa to launch a second round of spiritual reforms following his defeat of Zerah the Ethiopian? (2 Chr. 15:1–7)

In what stages did King Asa accomplish a thorough reform of Judah, including territory and subjects recently acquired from Israel? (2 Chr. 15:8–17)

The numbers 35 and 36 in 2 Chronicles 15:19 and 16:1 probably should read 25 and 26 respectively. King Baasha of Israel died in the twenty-sixth year of Asa's reign (see 1 Kin. 16:8). In what would be the final year of his life, Baasha started fortifying Ramah in the territory of Benjamin to halt the flow of spiritual refugees from Israel to Judah (see 2 Chr. 15:9). How did King Asa respond to this new military threat from Israel? (1 Kin. 15:18–22; 2 Chr. 16:2–6)

How did the Lord react to Asa's reliance on the Syrians to deliver Judah from Israel's pressure? (2 Chr. 16:7–9)

KINGDOM EXTRA

Scripture maintains a consistent testimony that the Lord searches continually and diligently for those whose hearts are fully devoted to Him so that He can bless them. Maintain a heart that is fully committed to the Lord. Know that the Lord seeks out such to strengthen them and to prosper their work.[5]

How did King Asa falter in his devotion to the Lord at the end of his reign? (2 Chr. 16:10–12)

At the time of his death, how did the people of Judah show their high regard for King Asa? (2 Chr. 16:13, 14)

FAITH ALIVE

What kinds of situations can make lukewarm believers (such as Rehoboam and Abijah) courageously trust in the Lord and experience impressive spiritual victories?

Why do those sorts of experiences seldom carry over into everyday dependence on the Lord and His Spirit?

In what circumstances of life do you think God wants us to rely on Him rather than on the resources of the world (as Asa did when Baasha fortified Ramah)?

VIOLENT GODLESSNESS

In Judah the spiritual issue was whether the descendants of David had the kind of heart for God that their famous ancestor had. In Israel the spiritual issue was whether a king could escape God's judgment and be succeeded by his son. The condition worsened until a true champion of wickedness emerged on the throne.

After becoming king, Jeroboam's son Nadab initiated an on-again, off-again twenty-four-year siege of the Philistine fortress Gibbethon (1 Kin. 15:27). What became of both Jeroboam's son and his hopes for a lasting dynasty? (1 Kin. 15:25–32)

The Lord sent a message to Baasha by means of Jehu (1 Kin. 16:1), whose father later prophesied to Asa (2 Chr. 16:7). What prophetic word did the Lord send to Baasha when he proved to be as wicked as the son of Jeroboam he replaced? (1 Kin. 16:1–4)

When he died, for what was Baasha remembered? (1 Kin. 16:5–7)

Little was said about Baasha, but he did reign twenty-four years (1 Kin. 15:33). His son Elah, like Jeroboam's son before, only lasted two years on the throne of Israel before disaster struck (16:8). What happened to Elah and his family and friends? (1 Kin. 16:9–14)

Twenty-four years after Nadab first besieged Gibbethon of Philistia (1 Kin. 15:27), the army of Israel was still at it (16:15). What happened when the army heard that Zimri had assassinated King Elah? (1 Kin. 16:16–20)

Clearly the political structure of Israel was unraveling. There was no legitimate government, and justice was degenerating into murder and revenge. It would be four more years before a strong central government emerged in Israel. What happened during those four years? (1 Kin. 16:21, 22)

What was King Omri's first move to stabilize his rule over the northern kingdom of Israel? (1 Kin. 16:23, 24)

King Omri was a powerful ruler, mentioned respectfully in extra-biblical history. The Assyrians ever after referred to Israel as "The House of Omri." How did the Lord assess the rule of this masterful politician? (1 Kin. 16:25–28)

Ahab, the son of Omri, introduced new evil into the life of Israel. He would become the adversary of Elijah and Elisha. The kingdom of darkness would battle the kingdom of light through these men—each mighty in his own way. How did Ahab surpass all the earlier kings of Israel in wickedness? (1 Kin. 16:29–34)

 BEHIND THE SCENES

Some Canaanite religions believed that houses, buildings, and city walls were inhabited by spirits. They would sacrifice the male child born closest to the start of construction and encase his corpse in the cornerstone so his spirit would animate the structure. Ancient Jewish traditions say Hiel gave two sons as human sacrifices to ensure the vitality of the new settlement at Jericho (1 Kin. 16:34).[6] Ahab's reign truly marked a degraded low in Israelite history if babies were blocked up in walls as part of idolatrous rituals.

 KINGDOM EXTRA

When God allowed His people to choose a king to rule them in His name, He saw to it that His Spirit moved prophets to guide and challenge the king to be true to God's Law. Obviously the prophets Elijah and Elisha dominate a large section of 1 and 2 Kings. Less obviously, other prophets play crucial roles in the lives of many of the kings. Nathan blessed the reigns of David and Solomon (2 Sam. 7:1–17; 12:1–25; 1 Kin. 1:8–45; 2 Chr. 9:29). So far in 1 Kings and 2 Chronicles, Ahijah the Shilonite (1 Kin. 11:29–39; 14:1–18; 2 Chr. 9:29), Shemaiah the man of God (1 Kin. 12:22–24; 2 Chr. 11:2–4; 12:5–8, 15), the man of God and the old prophet of Bethel

(1 Kin. 13), Jehu the son of Hanani (1 Kin. 16:1–7), Azariah the son of Oded the prophet (2 Chr. 15:1–8), Hanani the seer (2 Chr. 16:7–10), and Iddo the seer (2 Chr. 9:29; 12:15; 13:22) have provided direct communication to kings—often erring kings—from the mouth of God.

The main role of the prophet was to bear God's word. Whether warning of impending danger or disclosing God's will to the king, they were similar in function to the modern preacher in the church.

The ministry of prophecy is still alive in the church (1 Cor. 14:29, 32; Eph. 4:11). To acknowledge the present office of a prophet is not to suggest the individual is a writer of Scripture. This ministry is primarily for stirring up and building up the church (Eph. 4:11, 12), *not* offering interesting forecasts. Prophetic ministry should have a base of accountability where the person's ministry is nourished, prayed for, and sent forth with accountability (Acts. 13:1–3; 14:26–28).[7]

 FAITH ALIVE

Why do you think godlessness and selfishness tend to result in violent behavior?

Why does God continue sending His Word to us when we are bent on turning away from Him? How do we judge ourselves when we reject His grace?

1. *Spirit-Filled Life® Bible* (Nashville: Thomas Nelson Publishers, 1991), 526, "Truth-in-Action through 1 Kings."

2. Ibid., 624, Map "A Kingdom Divided."

3. Ibid., 1367–8, "Word Wealth, Zech. 3:8, wondrous sign."

4. J. Barton Payne, "1, 2 Chronicles," *The Expositor's Bible Commentary,* Vol. 4 (Grand Rapids: Zondervan Publishing House, 1988), 480.

5. *Spirit-Filled Life® Bible,* 654, "Truth-in-Action through 2 Chronicles."

6. R. D. Patterson and Hermann J. Austel, "1, 2 Kings," *The Expositor's Bible Commentary,* Vol. 4, 137.

7. *Hayford's Bible Handbook* (Nashville: Thomas Nelson Publishers, 1995), 736, "Prophet."

The Glory of the Prophets
1 Kings 17:1—2 Kings 8:15;
2 Chronicles 17:1—21:3

First Kings 18:12 is the only direct reference to the Holy Spirit in 1 Kings, where He is called the "Spirit of the LORD." King Ahab's steward Obadiah indicated that the Holy Spirit sometimes transported Elijah from one location to another.

There is also an allusion in 1 Kings 18:46 ("the hand of the LORD") to the Holy Spirit enabling Elijah to perform miracles. The formula "hand of the LORD" usually referred to the inspiration of the prophets by the Spirit of God. Here it applied to the Spirit of God as the agent who endowed Elijah with supernatural strength to do an amazing feat.[1]

When King Ahab and Queen Jezebel of the northern kingdom of Israel promoted the worst imaginable forms of wickedness, God responded with His mightiest prophetic messages and wonders. The Lord's glory shone brightest through His prophets Elijah and Elisha when the king of Israel led the Lord's people into sin and shame. The spiritual warfare was intense, and the Lord's victory enhanced His glory for all to see then and now.

Lesson 5/The Power of Glory
1 Kings 17—20
(874—853 B.C.)[2]

The world was moved in 1956 when five missionaries were speared to death in Ecuador while trying to make contact with a primitive tribe of people called the Auca. More moving was the subsequent evangelization of the Auca by the widows of two of the martyred missionaries. Most amazing was the movement of God's Spirit among the Auca to bring many of them to faith in Christ—including the young men who had participated in the ambush and massacre.

Nearly forty years passed before the story of that tragic day was told from the side of attackers. They now call themselves Huaorani (The People) instead of Auca (Savages). The attack on the missionaries occurred because a young girl tried to hide her involvement with a villager by saying the missionaries had attacked her. The killings were an act of revenge by a group of six Auca—five of them teenagers.

The Auca attackers reported they repeatedly speared the armed missionaries who protested but did not defend themselves. As the killings went on a shining choir appeared above the treetops and sang songs the Auca did not understand. Some only saw moving lights, but all heard the songs.

The Auca burned their village and fled into the jungle to hide, but they never forgot the strangers who did not defend themselves or the supernatural choir that hymned the martyrs home. They were ready to respond in faith when the gospel of Jesus Christ made sense of both vivid memories.[3]

POWER TO WITHHOLD OR GIVE

At first the glory of God acted powerfully but privately through the prophet Elijah. He experienced stretches of obscurity punctuated by moments of public confrontation with King Ahab. Subsequent events may indicate that Elijah preferred the safety of obscurity to the danger of notoriety.

Locate the hometown and home territory of Elijah on the following map.

ELIJAH AND ELISHA[4]

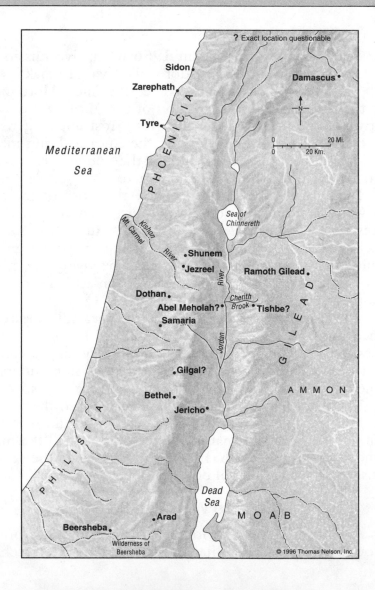

The Bible introduces Elijah not in his first contact with King Ahab but in one when the patience of God had expired with the wicked king of the northern kingdom of Israel. What message of power did the Lord send to Ahab through Elijah? (1 Kin. 17:1)

While God displayed His power on a cosmic scale to chasten rebellious King Ahab, how did He direct His power on a personal level to care for His prophet Elijah? (1 Kin. 17:2–6)

When the Brook Cherith dried up from the drought, where did the Lord direct Elijah to go to be safe from King Ahab? (1 Kin. 17:7–9)

What was the irony of God concealing Elijah in the territory of Sidon? (compare 1 Kin. 16:31 and 17:9)

How would you characterize the widow of Zarephath from the way she responded to the requests of the stranger from Israel who asked her for water and bread? (1 Kin. 17:10–12)

In how many ways did the Lord's words through Elijah challenge the faith of the widow from Zarephath? (1 Kin. 17:13–16)

KINGDOM EXTRA

This episode teaches us to invite God to work by His unlimited power within our limited circumstances and resources. Two important principles for our giving are illustrated by this passage of Scripture. First, we must give something out of our need. That is the kind of giving that involves our faith. Second, we must give first as a way of activating the miracle supply of God.

Your giving causes something to happen according to God's eternal principles of seedtime and harvest. There is an old saying: "Without God, you cannot; without you, God will not." God has already given from His side. Now we must step out in our giving to Him.[5]

How did the widow from Zarephath interpret the death of her only son? (1 Kin. 17:17, 18)

How did Elijah go about interceding for the dead son of the widow who had cared for him during the drought and famine? (1 Kin. 17:19–21)

Parallel the stages of the restoration of physical life to the son to the restoration of spiritual hope to his mother. (1 Kin. 17:22–24)

KINGDOM EXTRA

Often we do not understand the reason for sickness. The widow of Zarephath questioned Elijah's responsibility (1 Kin. 17:18); Elijah questioned God's reasonableness (v. 18); then lying prostrate on the child, he cried out in intercession to the Lord (v. 21)—and resurrection was the result. Healing comes as we move from reasoning over questions of *why* and begin responding to *how* the Lord works through faith-filled prayer. The Lord desires to heal.[6]

What could have happened for King Ahab if he had responded to the drought in the same way the widow responded to the death of her son?

FAITH ALIVE

How have you seen God withhold His blessing from you or from another in order to make His displeasure with sin obvious?

How have you seen God bestow His blessing on you or on another in order to express His good pleasure with growing faith?

POWER TO CONQUER EVIL

The drought and resultant famine did not move King Ahab and Queen Jezebel to turn from idolatry to the Lord. When their hearts were obviously hardened against Him, God turned from patient waiting for repentance to direct confrontation with the sinners.

In the New Testament, James says the famine lasted three and a half years (James 5:17). How did Elijah know the time had come for the drought to end? (1 Kin. 18:1)

What was the situation like throughout Israel because of the drought? (1 Kin. 18:2, 5)

What had been Queen Jezebel's response to the drought which God had sent to cause her to repent of her idolatry? (1 Kin. 18:4a)

What had been King Ahab's response to the drought which God had sent to cause him to repent of his idolatry? (1 Kin. 18:10)

What kind of man was King Ahab's chief steward Obadiah? (1 Kin. 18:4, 7, 9–13)

What were Ahab and Obadiah doing when the Lord told Elijah the drought was going to end? (1 Kin. 18:3–6)

Why was Obadiah reluctant to take the message to King Ahab that Elijah had been found? (1 Kin. 18:7–14)

Obadiah accepted Elijah's oath in the name of the Lord of hosts and delivered the message of the prophet's reappearance to King Ahab (1 Kin. 18:15). From Ahab's point of view, how was Elijah the "troubler of Israel"? (1 Kin. 18:17)

In fact, how had Ahab and his ancestors troubled Israel for generations? (1 Kin. 18:18)

Who did Elijah tell Ahab to assemble on Mount Carmel, and what issue did the prophet want the people to decide? (1 Kin. 18:19–21)

What was the contest Elijah proposed on Mount Carmel? Who was on the opposing sides? (1 Kin. 18:22–24)

How did the prophets of Baal attempt to get their god to respond to their sacrifice? (1 Kin. 18:25–29)

BEHIND THE SCENES

The original readers of 1 Kings understood certain aspects of the story that we don't. They knew that Baal was a fertility god who supposedly controlled the rain. Lightning was one of his trademarks. When the Lord stopped the rains by Elijah's command, He showed Baal's impotence. When Baal did not send fire on the altar of his priests and the Lord did, the Lord won again on Baal's home court. When He sent the rains shortly after, the evidence was overwhelming. There is only one true and living God.

What do you think it meant to Elijah's audience that he made the altar of the Lord from twelve stones and named it Israel? (1 Kin. 18:30, 31)

What did each of these add to the glory of the Lord's display of power on Mount Carmel?

• The way Elijah prepared the sacrifice (1 Kin. 18:32–35)

• The way Elijah called on the Lord (1 Kin. 18:36, 37)

• The way the Lord consumed the sacrifice (1 Kin. 18:38)

What was the response of the people of Israel to the Lord's demonstration of His glorious power on Mount Carmel? (1 Kin. 18:39, 40)

What did each of these men do after Elijah announced God's message that the rains were within earshot? (1 Kin. 18:41, 42)

• King Ahab

- Elijah, the prophet of God

Why do you think God wanted Elijah to engage in earnest prayer before He sent the already-promised rain? (1 Kin. 18:42–44)

KINGDOM EXTRA

Much can be learned about prayer from observing Elijah. First, even though we have a promise for God's provision, we are not to stop praying for its fulfillment. Second, we see one of the postures of prayer as he bowed with his head between his knees. Third, we learn the importance of persistence in prayer as we read that Elijah prayed seven times. And fourth, we understand the necessity of faith as we pray by realizing that Elijah believed his prayer was answered before the answer actually came.[7]

What do you think it meant to everyone involved that Elijah outran Ahab's chariot through the pouring rain to Jezreel, more than fifteen miles away? (1 Kin. 18:45, 46)

What kind of empowerment do you think the Bible has in mind when it says "the hand of the LORD came upon Elijah"? (1 Kin. 18:46)

FAITH ALIVE

When have you been called on to stand pretty much alone against evil around you? How did the Lord sustain you in that situation?

What lessons about persistent praying for the will of God does Elijah's example teach you? (see also James 5:17, 18)

POWER TO REVIVE THE DOWNHEARTED

Elijah must have been thrilled to see the Lord demonstrate His glory with such power while humiliating the prophets of Baal on Mount Carmel. His adrenaline rush from that confrontation and his footrace with Ahab's chariot to Jezreel through the rain must have been exhilarating. Better still had to be witnessing the people of Israel turning to faith in the Lord as a mass. In his heart he must have hoped for the conversion of King Ahab and Queen Jezebel to trust in the Lord. When that finally didn't happen, Elijah's ecstasy turned to despair.

What was King Ahab's reaction to what the Lord did on Mount Carmel? (1 Kin. 19:1)

What was Queen Jezebel's reaction to what the Lord did on Mount Carmel? (1 Kin. 19:2)

How did the hero of Mount Carmel react to the death threat of Queen Jezebel? (1 Kin. 19:3, 4)

How did the Lord respond to Elijah's prayer that he might die? (1 Kin. 19:5–8)

 BEHIND THE SCENES

Mount Horeb was another name for Mount Sinai. God directed Elijah to the place where He had made His covenant with Israel. Literally, the Hebrew says Elijah entered "*the cave*" (1 Kin. 19:9). Many commentators speculate this was "the cleft of the rock" (Ex. 33:22) from which Moses saw the Lord's back and received courage to lead the people of Israel after they worshiped the golden calf.[8]

How did Elijah explain his flight all the way from Samaria in Israel to Horeb in the Sinai peninsula? (1 Kin. 19:9, 10)

Why do you think the Lord revealed Himself to Elijah at that time and that place in "a still small voice" rather than in the wind, earthquake, or fire? (1 Kin. 19:11–13)

Why do you think the Lord responded to Elijah's second expression of self-pity with a new job to do? (1 Kin. 19:13–18)

In how many ways did the Lord show patience with Elijah's discouragement before it was time to give the prophet something new and challenging to do for Him? (1 Kin. 19:3–18)

In the light of all that had happened recently, why did the Lord begin a pattern of judgment on Israel through Hazael, Jehu, and Elisha? (1 Kin. 19:17)

Hazael of Syria became Israel's greatest enemy. Jehu, son of Nimshi, carried out the Lord's punishment of Ahab's family. Elisha succeeded Elijah as chief prophetic spokesman for the Lord to the kings of Israel. As Elijah traveled north from Mount Horeb, Abel Meholah was on his way home. What do you learn about Elisha from his first encounter with Elijah? (1 Kin. 19:19–21)

How did the Lord train Elisha to be a prophet of the same heroic mold as Elijah? (1 Kin. 19:19–21)

 ### FAITH ALIVE

What kinds of setbacks in life leave you discouraged? Are you easily discouraged or can you ignore many of life's lesser setbacks?

The Lord did several things in response to Elijah's discouragement. How do you think each of these helps the condition?

- Rest

- Good nutrition

- Spiritual comfort

- Something useful to do

Elijah had to get all the way back to Mount Sinai to get a restoring glimpse of God. What places or events from your spiritual journey or church history could you use as reference points to counteract discouraging influences in your life?

POWER TO REBUKE THE HALFHEARTED

The power of God worked patiently on behalf of Elijah, even when he was downhearted. But the power of God had no patience with King Ahab, who wanted to serve Baal with his wife and claim at the same time to be a follower of the Lord. This spiritual nonsense left Ahab insensitive to the will of God and open to His judgment.

The old king of Syria, Ben-Hadad, brought a force of thirty-two city-kings and their armies, along with horses and chariots, to besiege King Ahab in Samaria (1 Kin. 20:1). What were the original terms of surrender that Ahab found acceptable? (1 Kin. 20:2–4)

What additional terms of surrender from the Syrian forces did Ahab and his advisers reject? (1 Kin. 20:5–9)

What was the diplomatic and military situation after Ahab refused Syrian officials permission to search Samaria and take anything they wanted? (1 Kin. 20:10–12)

How did King Ahab respond initially to the prophet of the Lord who promised deliverance from the Syrian siege force? (1 Kin. 20:13–15)

How did the battle unfold between the Israelite liberators and the Syrian siege force? (1 Kin. 20:16–21)

What promise did the prophet of the Lord give Ahab after Samaria was liberated from the Syrians? (1 Kin. 20:22)

What was the Syrian strategy following their defeat at Samaria? (1 Kin. 20:23–25)

What was the battle situation the following spring when the new Syrian army set up base camp at Aphek in the plains of Israel? (1 Kin. 20:26, 27)

What message did the Lord send through "a man of God" (evidently a different prophet from the year before) to Ahab about the invading Syrians? (1 Kin. 20:28)

What was the outcome of the battle on the plains near Aphek? (1 Kin. 20:29, 30)

What was the political outcome of the defeat of the second Syrian army by the divinely aided forces of Israel? (1 Kin. 20:31–34)

Yet a third prophet of the Lord, one of the "sons of the prophets," now brought another message to King Ahab from the Lord. What are the first clues that the message from the Lord to Ahab is not a pleasant one? (1 Kin. 20:35–37)

The disguised prophet pretended to be a wounded soldier who had been charged to guard a prisoner with his life. Supposedly the prisoner had escaped and the soldier feared being executed for dereliction of duty. The king had no sympathy for a soldier who had let a prisoner get away (1 Kin. 20:38–40). How did the prophet apply his mini-drama to King Ahab? (1 Kin. 20:41, 42)

How did King Ahab react to the well-deserved rebuke of the prophet of God? (1 Kin. 20:43)

 BEHIND THE SCENES

The "sons of the prophets" was a designation for an association of prophets-in-training during the time of the monarchy. This is the first use of this title for this band of prophets, although they probably appeared in the story of King Saul's coronation (1 Sam. 10:9–13). "Son" did not imply physical relationship, but spiritual relationship. Young prophets associated with experienced prophets for account-ability, discipleship, and apprenticeship. Elisha especially invested time and energy in ministering to these younger prophets.

     FAITH ALIVE

Why does God continue to extend His grace to unbe-lievers and backsliders when it seems as though they have no intention of responding to Him in faith?

When do you think the patience of the Lord ends with the unrepentant and His judgment begins?

What should you learn from the attitudes and behavior of the Lord in terms of your own response to unbelievers and backsliders?

1. *Hayford's Bible Handbook* (Nashville: Thomas Nelson Publishers, 1995), 82, "Keys to 1 Kings."

2. Dates of King Ahab's reign.

3. Steve Saint, "Did They Have to Die?" *Christianity Today* (September 16, 1996), 20–27.

4. *Spirit-Filled Life® Bible* (Nashville: Thomas Nelson Publishers, 1991), 518, map "Elijah and Elisha."

5. Ibid., 514, "Kingdom Dynamics, 1 Kin. 17:8–16, You Must Give God an Opportu-nity."

6. *Hayford's Bible Handbook*, 86, "Surveying 1 Kings."

7. *Spirit-Filled Life® Bible*, 516, 517, note on 1 Kin. 18:41–45.

8. Donald J. Wiseman, *1 and 2 Kings: An Introduction and Commentary* (Leicester, England: InterVarsity Press, 1993), 172. Richard D. Patterson and Hermann L. Austel, "1, 2 Kings," *The Expositor's Bible Commentary*, Vol. 4 (Grand Rapids: Zondervan Publishing House, 1988), 149.

Lesson 6/The Humility of Glory
1 Kings 21—2 Kings 1;
2 Chronicles 17:1—21:3
(874—847 B.C.)[1]

"Power corrupts," the old saying goes, "and absolute power corrupts absolutely."

Perhaps a new saying could go: "Glory humbles, and absolute glory humbles absolutely."

When the queen of Sheba saw the splendor of Solomon's court, "there was no more spirit in her" (1 Kin. 10:1-5). When the prophet Isaiah had a vision in the temple and saw the Lord in all His glory attended by the seraphim, he detested his own sinfulness (Isa. 6:1-5). When the apostle John was in the Spirit on the island of Patmos and saw the resurrected Lord Jesus, he fell at His feet as though dead (Rev. 1:10-17).

After Job challenged the Lord to justify the suffering he was enduring, the Lord appeared to him. All Job could say after seeing the glory of God was, "I have heard of you by the hearing of the ear, / But now my eye sees You. / Therefore I abhor myself, / And repent in dust and ashes" (Job 42:5, 6).

In 1 and 2 Kings and 2 Chronicles, the prophets of God kept the kings of Israel and Judah aware of the glory of God. The wise kings responded in humility.

HUMILITY OF REPENTANCE

King Ahab was a thoroughly despicable man. He ruined himself and his people with idolatry. He let his evil wife Queen Jezebel dominate him. He pouted when he didn't get his way. He hated the prophets of God—killing many and hounding

Elijah relentlessly. But remarkably, when Ahab sank to his worst, the glory of God's prophetic word wrung repentance from even his hard heart.

Describe the situation and the disagreement that provide the setting for 1 Kings 21. (vv. 1–3)

📖 BIBLE EXTRA

Read Leviticus 25:23–28 and Numbers 36:7–9 and explain why Naboth the Jezreelite did not want to sell his vineyard or exchange it for a better one.

How did King Ahab respond to Naboth's refusal to sell his vineyard? What does this reveal about the king of Israel? (1 Kin. 21:4, compare 20:43)

How did Jezebel contrast with Ahab in her approach to problems? (1 Kin. 21:5–7)

How did Queen Jezebel go about solving the problem created by Naboth's refusal to sell King Ahab his vineyard adjacent to the royal residence in Jezreel? (1 Kin. 21:8–10)

What kind of guilt would you assign to each of these in the murder-disguised-as-execution of Naboth the Jezreelite? (1 Kin. 21:7–14)

- The two scoundrels who gave false testimony

- The elders and nobles who carried out Jezebel's orders

- Queen Jezebel, who devised and ordered the murder

- King Ahab, who closed his eyes but loaned his name to it all

How did Queen Jezebel and King Ahab react to the execution/murder of Naboth? (1 Kin. 21:15, 16)

How did the Lord and Elijah His prophet react to the exccution/murder of Naboth? (1 Kin. 21:17–19)

How had King Ahab's perception of the prophet Elijah changed in the time since the drought and famine? (compare 1 Kin. 21:20 with 18:17)

Because of the abuse of royal power in ordering Naboth's execution, what was God's sentence on each of these?
- King Ahab (1 Kin. 21:19, 21)

- King Ahab's descendants (1 Kin. 21:21, 22, 24)

- Queen Jezebel (1 Kin. 21:23)

What was the final biblical assessment of the overall reign of King Ahab and Queen Jezebel? (1 Kin. 21:25, 26)

In spite of Ahab's great wickedness and its far-reaching, long-lasting effects on Israel and Judah, what surprising results arose from this encounter of King Ahab with the glorious power of Elijah's prophetic word from God? (1 Kin. 21:27–29)

FAITH ALIVE

When in the past have you been moved to recognize your own sinfulness because you have glimpsed the glory of God's holiness and power?

How in the past have you sensed the Spirit of God using the power of the Word of God to convict you of sin?

HUMILITY OF THE TRUTH

The glory of God that shone through the prophecy of Elijah caused King Ahab to respond humbly in repentance. The glory of God that shone through the prophecy of Micaiah forced King Ahab of Israel and King Jehoshaphat of Judah to humble themselves before the truth. One king humbled himself while in terror he might die, the other while his life ebbed away.

What precipitated the next conflict between the northern kingdom of Israel and its Syrian neighbors farther to the northeast? (1 Kin. 22:2, 3)

Why did Jehoshaphat agree so readily to ally Judah with Ahab and Israel against Syria? (1 Kin. 22:4; 2 Chr. 18:1–3)

What was the difference between the approaches of the two kings in discerning the will of God about the impending battle with the Syrians? (1 Kin. 22:5–8; 2 Chr. 18:4–7)

Describe the scene into which Micaiah the prophet was brought from prison to prophesy. (1 Kin. 22:9–12; 2 Chr. 18:8–11)

Why do you think Micaiah gave Ahab a sarcastic prophecy promising him success at Ramoth Gilead? (1 Kin. 22:13–16; 2 Chr. 18:12–15)

What did Micaiah the prophet reveal to Ahab in each of his vision reports?
1. The sheep without a shepherd (1 Kin. 22:17; 2 Chr. 18:16)

2. The lying spirit (1 Kin. 22:18–23; 2 Chr. 18:17–22)

 BEHIND THE SCENES

Ahab and the false prophets wanted to believe a lie more than they really wanted the Lord's will. God is not the father of lies; the devil is (John 8:44). So God permitted an evil spirit to accomplish what Satan is always intent on doing.[2]

What was the response of King Ahab and his horde of false prophets to Micaiah's message? (1 Kin. 22:24–28; 2 Chr. 18:23–27)

How did each of these factors fit together to fulfill the prophetic Word of the Lord through Micaiah? (1 Kin. 22:29–34; 2 Chr. 18:28–33)
- The protective scheme of Ahab and Jehoshaphat

- The strategy of the Syrian leaders

- What appeared to be a random incident

When do you think each of these kings realized that the prophetic word they had heard from the Lord was the truth which he should have paid more attention to?

- King Jehoshaphat of Judah

- King Ahab of Israel

How were these prophecies fulfilled by the battle between the Israelites and Syrians at Ramoth Gilead? (1 Kin. 22:35–38; 2 Chr. 18:34)

- Micaiah's vision of sheep without a shepherd (see 1 Kin. 22:17)

- Micaiah's vision of the lying spirit (see 1 Kin. 22:20–23)

- Elijah's prediction of Ahab's death (see 1 Kin. 21:19)

 FAITH ALIVE

Why do you think so many people today—even some in the church—have little or no respect for the truth of God's Word?

How does the truth of God's Word end up humbling those who ignore it and live according to a lie?

What aspect of the truth of God's Word are you tempted to ignore in favor of selfish ends? How can you affirm your resolve to humble yourself before the truth?

HUMILITY OF PRAISE

Typically we think of praise as an uplifting spiritual experience. There are times, however, when our praise reminds us of how high above us the Lord God is and our praise humbles us before His majesty. King Jehoshaphat had an experience in which praise opened the way for the power of God to deliver him. That kind of praise humbles a person too.

You will notice that 1 Kings has little to say about Jehoshaphat, even though he was one of the most righteous kings of Judah. The author of 1 Kings focused on King Ahab and the prophets who opposed him to the virtual exclusion of Jehoshaphat. The chronicler, however, devoted four chapters to Jehoshaphat.

In the summary of Jehoshaphat's reign given in 1 Kings 22:41–50, what are the accomplishments and failures listed? (see also 2 Chr. 20:31–37)

- Accomplishments

- Failures

How did the chronicler assess the spiritual quality of the early portion of King Jehoshaphat's reign over Judah? (2 Chr. 17:3–9)

What was the political and military situation for Judah in the early portion of King Jehoshaphat's twenty-five year reign? (2 Chr. 17:1, 2, 10–19)

King Jehoshaphat's campaign with King Ahab of Israel against Ramoth Gilead separated an early time of enthusiasm for the Lord from a second, renewed zeal for Him. How did the Lord get Jehoshaphat's attention so that the king became eager to serve Him again? (2 Chr. 19:1–3)

What innovations in the countryside did King Jehoshaphat make in his second round of reforms in Judah? (2 Chr. 19:4–7)

What innovations did King Jehoshaphat make in the city of Jerusalem? (2 Chr. 19:8–11)

In these reforms, how did justice and godliness complement one another? (2 Chr. 19:4–11)

Make a list of the qualities necessary for justice King Jehoshaphat commended to the various judges he appointed. Why is justice so hard to administer fairly? (2 Chr. 19:7, 9, 11)

What situation developed to test the depth of Jehoshaphat's commitment to the Lord? (2 Chr. 20:1, 2)

 BEHIND THE SCENES

Verse 2 says the massive invading army came from Syria. The Hebrew words for Syria and Edom are extremely similar. *Aram* and *Edom* differ only in the middle consonant when written without vowels as Semitic languages are. The difference between the "r" and the "d" characters in Hebrew is the little tail or serif that Jesus referred to as a "tittle"—the smallest part of a letter (Matt. 5:18). It appears in 2 Chronicles 20 that the invaders came from Edom rather than Syria and that an ancient scribe confused the names.

How did King Jehoshaphat prepare to face the threat of the invading armies from Moab, Ammon, and their allies? (2 Chr. 20:3–5)

How did Jehoshaphat pray about each of these topics? (2 Chr. 20:5–13)

- The character of God

- The temple

- The invaders

 KINGDOM EXTRA

Fasting was one of the keys to releasing the deliverance Judah experienced. This was a proclaimed fast in which the whole nation participated. Fasting is not a tool by which one manipulates God to accomplish something. Fasting is simply an outward indication of an inward sincerity, evidence of the urgency we feel when praying for special needs.

A second key integral to Judah's deliverance was prayer. Verse 12 gives the essence of the prayer of helplessness. "For we have no power . . . nor do we know what to do, but our eyes are upon you." The cry of Christians in the darkest night of their experience is: "Lord, I do not know what to do, but I am counting on You."[3]

What message did the Spirit of the Lord give Jahaziel the Levite? (2 Chr. 20:14–17)

How did the king and his subjects respond to the prophetic promise of deliverance from their invading enemies? (2 Chr. 20:18, 19)

How did King Jehoshaphat and the people of Israel go out to meet the invading armies of Moab, Ammon, and Edom? (2 Chr. 20:19–21)

 KINGDOM EXTRA

Man was created to live and breathe in an atmosphere of praise-filled worship to his Creator. The avenue of sustained inflow of divine power was to be kept by the sustained outflow of joyous and humble praise to his Maker. Upon receiving Jesus Christ as Savior, daily living calls us to prayer and the Word for fellowship and wisdom in living. Our daily approach to God in that communion is to be paved with praise: "Enter into His gates with thanksgiving, and into His courts with praise" (Ps. 100:4). Such a walk of praise-filled openness to Him will cultivate deep devotion, faithful obedience, and constant joy.[4]

What happened to the invading Moabites, Ammonites, and Edomites when the choirs of Judah began praising the Lord and the beauty of holiness? (2 Chr. 20:22–25)

How did King Jehoshaphat and the "army" of Judah conclude their "battle" against the invaders from Moab, Ammon, and Edom? (2 Chr. 20:26–28)

KINGDOM EXTRA

As Judah began to sing and praise God with the expectancy that He would fight for them, their enemies were defeated. Similar praise-induced victories occur in Joshua 6:10, 20; Judges 7:18–22; 2 Kings 7:3–16; and 19:35. Psalm 22:3 explains that God is enthroned in the praises of His people. Whenever and wherever God's people praise Him, He reigns among them and does miraculous things on their behalf.[5]

What were the long-term results of the victory of Judah and Jehoshaphat over their enemies by means of singing the praise of the Lord? (2 Chr. 20:29, 30)

Second Kings records a later war with Moab in which Jehoshaphat allied himself with King Jehoram of Israel. Read 2 Kings 3:1–27. How did the lessons Jehoshaphat learned during the earlier war help prevent disaster for the combined armies of Israel and Judah?

FAITH ALIVE

What are your favorite songs of praise that you sing at church or in your personal worship? How do those songs humble you before the exalted Lord as one totally dependent on Him?

What difficulties and struggles are you facing now that are opportunities in which you can practice the holy warfare of praising the Lord and the beauty of holiness? How can you exercise praise in these circumstances?

HUMILITY OF JUDGMENT

While Judah was blessed with the reign of Jehoshaphat, Israel was cursed with the reign of Ahab's son Ahaziah. King Ahaziah experienced the glory of God through the ministry of the prophet Elijah. Ahaziah was not wise enough to respond to God's glory, but he had an army officer who did humble himself in the face of the fierce judgment of God.

What were the general characteristics of the reign of King Ahaziah over the northern kingdom of Israel? (1 Kin. 22:51—2 Kin. 1:1)

Ahaziah's reign was brief because he experienced tragedy early in his reign when he fell through the lattice-work window on the second story of his house in Samaria (2 Kin. 1:2). What were the missions of the two messengers dispatched because of Ahaziah's accident?

- The messenger Ahaziah sent (2 Kin. 1:2)

- The messenger the Lord sent (2 Kin. 1:3, 4)

King Ahaziah seems to have suspected that it was Elijah the Tishbite who had intercepted his messenger. Why do you think the king suspected it had been Elijah? (2 Kin. 1:5–7)

How did the messenger identify the unknown prophet of doom as Elijah? (2 Kin. 1:7, 8)

From the way the story unfolds, what seems to have been the reason for sending an officer with fifty soldiers to find Elijah? (2 Kin. 1:9)

What was the message the Lord was sending to King Ahaziah when He twice sent fire from heaven to consume the fifty-man squads sent to arrest His prophet Elijah? (2 Kin. 1:9–12)

Why didn't the Lord direct Elijah to call down fire to consume the third officer with his squad of soldiers? (2 Kin. 1:13–15)

What was the outcome of King Ahaziah's indifference to the Lord and His prophet Elijah? (2 Kin. 1:17, 18)

 FAITH ALIVE

When you sense the Lord's displeasure with some sin in your life, which of these is your typical first response?

  a. Anger that He would oppose my will.
  b. Frustration with the restrictive nature of holiness.
  c. Hope that no one finds out I've been sinning.
  d. Interest in lining up my life with God's ways.
  e. Sorrow that I have offended my Lord.

What is the most serious chastening from God you have experienced because of sin? What did you learn from it?

1. Dates from the start of Ahab's reign in Israel to the end of Jehoshaphat's reign in Judah.
2. *Spirit-Filled Life® Bible* (Nashville: Thomas Nelson Publishers, 1991), 523, note on 1 Kin. 22:15–23.
3. Ibid., 632, notes on 2 Chr. 20:3 and 20:4–11.
4. *Hayford's Bible Handbook* (Nashville: Thomas Nelson Publishers, 1995), 721, "Praise, The Pathway of."
5. *Spirit-Filled Life® Bible,* 633, note on 2 Chronicles 20:22, 23.

Lesson 7/ Passing on the Glory
2 Kings 2:1—8:15
(852—841 B.C.)[1]

Can there be a more conservative sport than baseball? When Lou Gehrig broke in with the Yankees in 1925, fans didn't like him because his success was a threat to Babe Ruth's status as the best in the game. In 1936 Joe DiMaggio became a threat to Gehrig. In 1951 Mickey Mantle was an unwelcome intruder in DiMaggio's last season.

In 1961 fans treated Roger Maris with thinly-veiled or open hostility as he hit sixty-one home runs to break Babe Ruth's record. They wanted to see the record broken, but they wanted Mickey Mantle to do it. He wore the hero's mantle—and had the name to prove it.

Long before he passed from the scene, Elijah had appointed Elisha his successor at the Lord's direction (1 Kin. 19:16, 19–21). Then Elijah mentored Elisha to assume the role of divine spokesman to the apostate kings of the northern kingdom of Israel. The Lord had no intention of leaving Israel without a strong witness to the truth; He loved them with an everlasting love. But would they accept Elisha with the same respect, fear, and (at times) hatred they showed Elijah?

IN THE POWER AND SPIRIT OF ELIJAH

The first thing the Lord did to ensure that Elisha would be accepted as His spokesman was arrange a dramatic transfer of authority witnessed by many people who would spread the word near and far. In fact, every time someone speaks of the mantle of office passing from one person to another, they are alluding to 2 Kings 2. Every time someone sings "Swing Low, Sweet Chariot," they are recalling Elijah's exit from and Elisha's entrance onto the stage of Old Testament history.

What role did each of these play in the unfolding drama of Elijah's departure from this life? (2 Kin. 2:1–7)

- Elijah

- Elisha

- The sons of the prophets

Circle the letter of what seems the most likely explanation of Elijah's repeated requests that Elisha let him go on alone. Explain your choice.

    a. Elijah was testing Elisha's commitment to being a prophet.
    b. Elijah didn't want to turn his departure into a self-promoting spectacle.
    c. Elijah didn't know that God wanted Elisha to witness his ascension. Only Elisha knew that.
    d. Elijah wanted to be alone with the Lord.

Why do you think Elijah wanted to visit each group of prophets in-training before his departure? (2 Kin. 2:3, 5, 7)

Why do you think the Lord had Elijah miraculously strike the Jordan River with his robe and cross over? (2 Kin. 2:8)

Why do you think the Lord, through Elijah, laid down a condition Elisha had to meet before he would be granted a double portion of the old prophet's spirit? (2 Kin. 2:9, 10)

BEHIND THE SCENES

The request for a double portion of Elijah's spirit was based on the custom that the firstborn son inherited a double share of his father's estate, while other sons received a single share each (Deut. 21:17). He was asking for empowerment to carry on the awesome task of speaking for the Lord in pressure-packed situations. The Hebrew word for **spirit** can refer to the human spirit, the Holy Spirit, an evil spirit, a prophetic gift, or even the wind. Even if it here refers to the spirit of prophecy that energized the ministry of Elijah, it ultimately requires the presence of the Holy Spirit as the author of Elijah's prophetic gift and ministry power.[2]

Describe Elijah's ascension into heaven and Elisha's reaction to it. (2 Kin. 2:11, 12)

What was the significance of Elisha crossing the Jordan as Elijah had? How important was the presence of the same witnesses at both events? (2 Kin. 2:14, 15; see v. 7)

Why didn't Elisha want the sons of the prophets looking for Elijah's body, and why did he give in to their request to search? (2 Kin. 2:16–18)

What did Elisha demonstrate about his power as a prophet when he purified the water of Jericho? (2 Kin. 2:19–22)

At Bethel, a center of apostate Israelite calf worship (1 Kin. 12:28, 29), a sizable gang of young toughs mocked Elisha and dared him to go up into heaven as Elijah had. Why do you think the Lord moved the prophet to punish them so severely? (2 Kin. 2:23, 24)

Why do you suppose the Lord directed Elisha to visit Mount Carmel before making his first solo appearance in Samaria, the capital of the northern kingdom of Israel? (2 Kin. 2:25; see 1 Kin. 17)

What was the good news and the bad news about the spiritual condition of Israel's King Jehoram, brother to King Ahaziah and son to King Ahab? (2 Kin. 3:1–3)

How did King Jehoram of Israel become allied with Jehoshaphat of Judah in a war against Moab? (2 Kin. 3:4–7)

Judah had defeated Edom in an earlier war and placed a puppet on the Edomite throne (2 Chr. 20; 1 Kin. 22:47). How did Judah's control of Edom factor into King Jehoram's battle plan against Moab? (2 Kin. 3:8–10)

Elisha the prophet seems to have travelled with the Israelite army from Samaria into the wilderness of Edom. What was his role in the battle of the kings of Israel and Judah against Moab? (2 Kin. 3:11–15)

How did the Lord provide for the armies of Israel and Judah to find water and defeat the Moabites? (2 Kin. 3:16–25)

What desperate measures did the king of Moab take that eventually disgusted the armies of Israel and Judah so much that they withdrew? (2 Kin. 3:26, 27)

FAITH ALIVE

What are the clearest evidences that a leader lives and serves in the Spirit and power of the Lord?

How have you seen the Lord confirm to His people that a new leader was one whom He wanted to shepherd them?

FOR THE HEALING OF MANY

The miracles of Elisha take on a different complexion than those of Elijah. Elisha's ministry was less confrontational and more helpful. Even when Elisha's miracles mirror those of Elijah, they don't have his flair. Instead they seem quiet and solid.

What were the needs and resources of the widow of one of the prophets-in-training? (2 Kin. 4:1, 2, 4)

How did the widow's faith lead her to a solution to her need? (2 Kin. 4:1, 2)

How did the widow's faith become the measure for the blessing she would receive? (2 Kin. 4:3–7)

KINGDOM EXTRA

Faith is, in essence, taking God at His Word and His Word at face value. God has a limitless supply of resources for all who trust in and obey Him. Fearing that we will not have enough in times of need insults the God who has revealed Himself as *Yahweh-Yireh,* The-Lord-Our-Provider.

Believe that God is able to supply your needs, even when you have no idea how. Know that God promises to keep His people alive in famine. This applies spiritually, too: God's spiritual resources for you are limitless, even during times of spiritual drought.[3]

How did Elisha come to have a close relationship with a wealthy woman from Shunem? (2 Kin. 4:8–10)

How did Elisha respond to the great kindness of the Shunammite woman and her husband? (2 Kin. 4:10–17)

How did the Shunammite woman respond to the tragic death of the son given her miraculously through the prophetic ministry of Elisha? (2 Kin. 4:11–28)

What steps did Elisha the prophet take to restore the dead child to life? What progression do you see in the steps? (2 Kin. 4:29–35)

What do you gather from the behavior of the woman of Shunem about her faith in God and His work through His prophet Elisha? (2 Kin. 4:21–30, 36, 37)

What concern did Elisha show for the daily needs of the prophets-in-training who looked up to him? (2 Kin. 4:38–41)

How did the Lord work through Elisha to extend the gifts of benefactors for the prophets-in-training? (2 Kin. 4:42–44)

Describe Naaman according to the following categories:

• His accomplishments (2 Kin. 5:1)

- His liability (2 Kin. 5:1)

- His presumed status in Israel

Why did Naaman go to Samaria with rich gifts and a letter to the king of Israel from the king of Syria asking that he be healed? (2 Kin. 5:2–6)

How did these two men respond to the letter requesting healing that Naaman brought to Samaria?

- The king (2 Kin. 5:7)

- Elisha (2 Kin. 5:8)

Why was Naaman offended by the way Elisha went about offering him a cure for his leprosy? (2 Kin. 5:9–12)

How was Naaman persuaded to follow the instructions of Elisha? (2 Kin. 5:13, 14)

What were Naaman's responses to the healing that God granted him through Elisha the prophet? (2 Kin. 5:15–18)

How did Gehazi's greed lead him into one sin after another? (2 Kin. 5:20–25)

How did Gehazi's punishment fit his crime? (2 Kin. 5:26, 27)

The miracles of Elisha associated with the sons of the prophets were intimate matters inside the brotherhood of teacher and students. What aspects of nature did God control through Elisha to do each of these?

- Make poisonous food nutritious (2 Kin. 4:38–41)

- Multiply bread to feed a crowd (2 Kin. 4:42–44)

- Make an iron ax head float (2 Kin. 6:1–7)

 BIBLE EXTRA

Jesus fulfills in the kingdom of God the roles of Prophet, Priest, and King. In the Old Testament, David typifies Jesus as King, Melchizedek typifies Jesus as Priest, and Elisha typifies Jesus as Prophet. Elijah plays a role too since John the Baptist ministered in the spirit of Elijah and Elijah appeared on the Mount of Transfiguration.

The miracles God worked through Elisha parallel the miracles of Jesus more than they parallel those of his mentor Elijah. In the list below, look up the Gospel verses and record the miracles of Jesus that align with those of Elisha.

ELISHA	JESUS
1 Succeeded Elijah (2 Kin. 2:1–15)	(Matt. 11:11–14; 17:1–13)
2 Associated with sons of the prophets (2 Kin. 4:38–44; 6:1–7)	(Mark 3:13–19; 6:7–13)
3 Multiplied food twice (2 Kin. 4:1–7, 42–44)	(Mark 6:30–44; 8:1–10)
4 Resurrected the widow's son (2 Kin. 4:32–37)	(Luke 7:11–17; 8:40–42, 49–56)
5 Healed a leper (2 Kin. 5:9–14)	(Luke 5:12–14; 17:11–19)

6 Healed by means   (John 9:1–7)
of washing (2 Kin.
5:10, 14)

7 Floated an ax head   (Matt. 14:28–31)
(2 Kin. 6:1–7)

 FAITH ALIVE

Because Jesus is the Prophet in the kingdom of God, it should surprise no one that He has sent the spirit of prophecy into that kingdom. Look up the following verses and summarize what each says about prophecy in the church.

*Acts 2:17–21

*1 Corinthians 14:1, 24, 25, 30–32; 1 Peter 4:11

*Ephesians 1:17–19

*Ephesians 2:19–22

*Ephesians 4:11–16

FOR THE DELIVERANCE OF GOD'S PEOPLE

The prophetic ministry of Elijah generally pronounced doom on the sinful court of King Ahab. Through Elisha the Lord spoke several messages of deliverance from the harassment by Syria, Israel's neighbor to the northeast. Unfortunately the king (who isn't even named in the report) responded to Elisha's word of deliverance no better than Ahab responded to Elijah's rebuke.

Israel and Syria had enjoyed a period of relatively peaceful relations, during which Naaman had visited the palace in

Samaria and Elisha's hometown as a guest of Israel. Later hostility erupted once more. What embarrassing situation did the King of Syria face as he tried to organize his offensive against Israel? (2 Kin. 6:8–11)

How did the king of Syria attempt to remedy his problem of military intelligence getting into Israelite hands? (2 Kin. 6:12–14)

How did Elisha comfort his agitated servant when he saw the encircling Syrian army? (2 Kin. 6:15–17)

 KINGDOM EXTRA

To believe the impossible one must first see the invisible—the lesson Elisha taught his servant. Elisha prayed, not that his servant would see a miracle, but that he would see another dimension. Seeing into the invisible is a key to victorious praying—discerning spiritual issues from God's perspective rather than man's, seeing the Adversary's attack plan, and perceiving God's angelic strike force.[4]

How did the prophet Elisha deal with the Syrian army that had been sent to take him prisoner? (2 Kin. 6:18–20)

How did the Lord direct the people of Israel to deal with the captured Syrian army? Why do you think He took this approach? (2 Kin. 6:21–23)

Extra-biblical sources indicate there were three Syrian kings named Ben-Hadad. Ben Hadad I frustrated Israel's attack on Judah in the days of King Asa (1 Kin. 15:16–22). Ben Hadad II waged intermittent war with King Ahab of

Israel (1 Kin. 20) and launched the very serious Syrian assault on Israel and its capital Samaria during the reign of Jehoram (2 Kin. 6:24—7:20). Ben Hadad III came along later during the reign of Jehoahaz (13:3). How serious were the siege conditions in Samaria created by the second Ben Hadad? (2 Kin. 6:24–29)

What was King Jehoram of Israel's first reaction to the deplorable situation in Samaria? (2 Kin. 6:30, 31) Why might he blame Elisha? (vv. 21–23)

The king seems to have changed his mind about killing Elisha and hurried after his messenger/executioner (2 Kin. 6:32). What conclusion had Jehoram reached about the siege of Samaria and any hope of deliverance by the Lord? (2 Kin. 6:33)

What predictions did Elisha make in the name of the Lord to the pessimistic king and his cynical officer? (2 Kin. 7:1, 2)

How did the Lord deliver Samaria, the capital of the northern kingdom of Israel, from the besieging army of the Syrians? (2 Kin. 7:6, 7)

How did the residents of Samaria discover that the Syrian army had abandoned its siege? (2 Kin. 7:3–5, 8–15)

How were all the details of Elisha's prophecy about the end of the Syrian siege of Samaria fulfilled? (2 Kin. 7:16–20)

FAITH ALIVE

What is the most dangerous situation you have faced in your life, and how did you find the Lord acting on your behalf during it?

When have you been tempted to doubt that God cared for you? How has He reassured you of His concern and His care for you?

FOR LIFE AND DEATH

Elisha's ministry extended the glory God had revealed through the heroic life of Elijah. The final two recorded incidents from Elisha's career as a prophet show him engaged in life-and-death work that exercised the double portion of Elijah's spirit that rested on him. Surely his was a glorious but challenging calling.

The woman from Shunem seems to have been widowed since the incidents of 2 Kings 4. Her husband isn't mentioned, and Elisha takes on a protective role for her. How did Elisha help her? (2 Kin. 8:1, 2)

What problem arose in her absence, and how did the Shunammite woman try to solve it? (2 Kin. 8:3) How does this approach fit with the image of this woman presented in 2 Kings 4:21–30?

When the Shunammite woman appeared in the court of the king of Israel, Elisha's former servant Gehazi was entertaining the king with stories about the prophet's exploits (2 Kin. 8:4, 5). How did Gehazi's witness about Elisha's deeds for the woman affect the king's response to her petition? (2 Kin. 8:5, 6)

At Mount Horeb the Lord had commissioned the prophet Elijah to anoint three men as successors to current leaders (1 Kin. 19:15–17). Elijah personally anointed one of the three—Elisha—as his own successor. Years later Elisha would complete Elijah's mission as his posthumous representative. What situation presented the occasion to deal with the first of the two remaining transitions? (2 Kin. 8:7, 8)

Describe Hazael's approach to Elisha and the prophet's very unusual response to him. (2 Kin. 8:9–11)

How did Elisha explain his rather bizarre answer and behavior to Hazael, the representative of the king of Syria? (2 Kin. 8:12, 13)

How did Hazael go about carrying out the prediction that the prophet Elisha had made about him? (2 Kin. 8:14, 15)

 FAITH ALIVE

Elisha was known as "the man of God" even in pagan Syria (2 Kin. 8:7). What kinds of things will establish our reputation as people of God among our unbelieving acquaintances?

Elisha probably rejoiced to know that he helped restore the livelihood of his friend, the Shunammite woman. He certainly grieved that his appointment of Hazael to the throne of Syria would cost many Israelite lives (v. 12). How does the Spirit-filled witness and service of every Christian bring life to some while announcing death to others? How do you feel about that?

1. Dates of King Joram/Jehoram of Israel.
2. *Spirit-Filled Life®Bible* (Nashville: Thomas Nelson Publishers, 1991), 531, 532, note on 2 Kin. 2:9–16.
3. Ibid., 569.
4. Ibid., 538, "Kingdom Dynamics, 2 Kin. 6:8–17, The Invisible Realm and Victorious Warfare."

The Inglorious End of Israel and Judah
2 Kings 8:16—25:30; 2 Chronicles 21:4—36:23

In a sense the life of King Joash of the southern kingdom of Judah mirrored the history of Israel and Judah. He began well under the tutelage of the high priest Jehoiada, but when the old priest died, King Joash began to follow the gods of the surrounding nations. Then the Lord raised up prophets to call Joash back to the truth, but Joash ordered the most vocal prophet stoned to death. As punishment, the Lord sent the Syrians to defeat Judah and Jerusalem. Joash was wounded in the battle and then killed by frustrated officials who disagreed with his policies.

Of the prophet Joash killed, the Bible says, "The Spirit of God came upon Zechariah the son of Jehoiada the priest" (2 Chr. 24:20). Literally the Hebrew reads, "The Spirit clothed Himself with Zechariah." The same amazing expression is used of Gideon's empowerment by the Holy Spirit (Judg. 6:34). As surely as the Lord clothed Himself with the faithful prophets, He would strip away from Himself the increasingly faithless kingdoms—first of Israel in the north and then Judah in the south.

Lesson 8/Despising the Glory
2 Kings 8:16—14:29;
2 Chronicles 21:4—25:28
(852—753 B.C.)

One hundred years ago Montgomery Ward was inventing the mail-order catalog and the money-back guarantee. It built a department-store empire of green-awninged buildings on Main Streets across the country. It prospered through the Great Depression because it had deep pockets and cautious management.

When World War II ended, cross-Chicago rival Sears Roebuck gambled everything it had on suburban shopping center stores. Montgomery Ward sneered at upstart Sears and promised to buy up the failed stores at pennies on the dollar. But Sears Roebuck had seen the future, and Montgomery Ward began its slide into retail oblivion.[1]

The kingdom of Israel blossomed when David and Solomon pursued the Lord wholeheartedly and made the temple the focus of their ambitions. After the people of God became prosperous, they assumed God would smile on anything they did. Increasingly, spiritual revivals became more superficial and short-lived. The legacy of Ahab and Jezebel corrupted both halves of God's people, and the slide into oblivion began. Even in Judah, attempts at reformation grew anemic.

A LITTLE LEAVEN LEAVENS THE WHOLE LUMP

The first two kings of the southern kingdom of Judah after Jehoshaphat show just how much influence King Ahab and Queen Jezebel of the northern kingdom of Israel had in the south even after their deaths. Ahab's daughter Athaliah married the son of Jehoshaphat and dominated her husband and son during their reigns before making herself queen after her son's untimely death. Indeed, a little leaven leavened the whole lump.

What do we learn about King Jehoram of Judah at the start of his reign that indicates he would be a wicked king? (2 Kin. 8:16–18; 2 Chr. 21:1–6)

What circumstance preserved Jehoram (and other evil kings of Judah) from experiencing divine judgment? (2 Kin. 8:19; 2 Chr. 21:7)

What was Jehoram's single notable accomplishment? (2 Kin. 8:20, 21; 2 Chr. 21:8, 9)

Despite that one victory, what was the political climate during Jehoram's reign? (2 Kin. 8:22; 2 Chr. 21:10, 16, 17)

Even though Elisha was the prophet in the limelight when Jehoram of Israel and Jehoshaphat of Judah attacked Moab through Edomite territory (2 Kin. 3:11–19), that event must have preceded Elijah's departure into heaven in the whirlwind (2:11), because he wrote a letter to Jehoshaphat's son Jehoram of Judah. What was the message of Elijah's letter? (2 Chr. 21:11–15)

What was the end of King Jehoram's life like? (2 Kin. 8:23, 24; 2 Chr. 21:18–20)

  BEHIND THE SCENES

Are you confused yet by the similar names of the kings of Israel and Judah? One more feature created by the inter-marriage between the son of Jehoshaphat of Judah and the daughter of Ahab of Israel was the duplication of names between the kingdoms. In this lesson, Israel's kings after Ahab were Ahaziah, Jehoram/Joram, Jehu, Jehoahaz, Jehoash/Joash, and Jeroboam II. In the same period, Judah's rulers after Jehoshaphat were Jehoram/Joram, Ahaziah, Queen Athaliah, Jehoash/Joash, and Amaziah. If it isn't bad enough that the same three names appear in both lists, they used long and short forms for two of them. At least the two Ahaziahs and Jehoash/Joashes didn't reign at the same time, but the two Jehoram/Jorams were contemporaries (852–841 B.C. in Israel and 848–841 B.C. in Judah).

What were the characteristics of the reign of Ahaziah, king of Judah? (2 Kin. 8:25–27; 2 Chr. 22:1–5)

What involvement with his uncle Joram of Israel paved the way for disaster for King Ahaziah of Judah? (2 Kin. 8:28, 29; 2 Chr. 22:5, 6)

After King Joram of Israel was wounded near Ramoth Gilead, an officer in the Israelite army led a coup against Joram (2 Kin. 9, 10). What happened to Ahaziah of Judah during this armed rebellion? (2 Kin. 9:27–29; 2 Chr. 22:7–9)

 FAITH ALIVE

At what point(s) in your life have you noticed that intimate contact with evil can desensitize you to the Spirit of God and open you up to temptation and sin?

How do you think you are to handle your friendships and contacts with unbelievers so that you can be an effective witness without being moved toward sin and worldliness?

BLOODY, PARTIAL OBEDIENCE

As Elijah's representative, Elisha arranged the anointing of Jehu as king of Israel (2 Kin. 9:1–3; see 1 Kin. 19:16). That act made Jehu Israel's only God-anointed king. He was assigned the task of ridding Israel of Baal worship and leading the northern kingdom back to the worship of the Lord. Jehu held in his hands the greatest opportunity of any king of Israel.

Who was this Jehu whom the Lord would make king of Israel? (2 Kin. 9:2, 24, 25)

Describe the anointing of Jehu to be king of Israel. (2 Kin. 9:1–6)

What charge from the Lord did the prophet-in-training give Jehu in conjunction with his anointing to be king of Israel? (2 Kin. 9:7–10; 2 Chr. 22:7)

How did the rest of the officers of the army of Israel respond to the news that Jehu had been anointed king over Israel by the prophet-in-training? (2 Kin. 9:11–15)

What kind of warning did Joram king of Israel have that he faced trouble from his army officer Jehu? (2 Kin. 9:16–20)

How did it come about that King Joram of Israel died on the plot of ground that his father King Ahab had stolen from Naboth of Jezreel? (2 Kin. 9:20–24)

What prophecies did Jehu have in mind when he left the unburied corpse of King Joram on the site of the vineyard of Naboth? (1 Kin. 21:19, 23, 24; 2 Kin. 9:7, 25, 26)

Jezebel, the queen mother of Israel, seems to have been still a powerful political and spiritual force in Israel. How did she react to the approach of Jehu who had just killed her son the king? (2 Kin. 9:30, 31)

What became of queen mother Jezebel in the security of her carefully guarded citadel? (2 Kin. 9:32–37)

Next Jehu turned his attention to the seventy members of the royal family (not literal "sons of Ahab") who could make various legitimate claims to the throne of Israel (2 Kin. 10:1). How did Jehu deal with them at a minimum of risk to himself or his armed supporters? (2 Kin. 10:1–8)

How was the way Jehu liquidated Ahab's family similar to the way he handled Jezebel? How did these strategies give Jehu power over those who helped him? (2 Kin. 10:9)

How did Jehu extend his annihilation of those with ties to Ahab to include even distant relatives? (2 Kin. 10:12–17)

How did Jehu next create a situation that would bring together all the Baal worshipers in Israel so he could deal with them? (2 Kin. 10:18–23)

How did Jehu effectively exterminate Baal worship from Israel in a single stroke? (2 Kin. 10:24–28)

How did God evaluate the reign of King Jehu, the one king of Israel anointed by a prophet of the Lord? (2 Kin. 10:29–31)

How did the Lord express his displeasure with Jehu's partial reforms of Israel during the remainder of his twenty-eight-year reign? (2 Kin. 10:32–36)

FAITH ALIVE

What do you think would happen in your life if you rooted out a life-dominating, bad habit but didn't fill the vacuum created by its absence with godly, Spirit-controlled behavior?

How can we tell, when we oppose evil forces and movements in the world, whether we are motivated by the Spirit of God or our own ambitions or desires?

THE GLORY OF A GODLY LEADER

Even as the kingdoms of Israel and Judah drifted away from the Lord under the influence of the descendants of Ahab and Judah, God intervened on behalf of His people. In Israel, the cure (in the person of Jehu) wasn't much better than the disease. In Judah, the Lord blessed his people with a remarkable monarch.

The daughter of King Ahab of Israel had been queen of Judah as the wife of Jehoram and queen mother of Judah as the mother of Ahaziah. After Jehu killed Ahaziah (2 Kin. 9:27), how did Athaliah treat her grandchildren and other tender relatives in the royal family? (2 Kin. 11:1; 2 Chr. 22:10)

How did the infant Joash survive the royal family massacre? (2 Kin. 11:2, 3; 2 Chr. 22:11, 12)

Apparently Queen Athaliah did not enjoy popular support, but reigned six years because there was no legitimate heir to challenge her claim to the throne. How did the high priest

Jehoiada plan to crown Joash king of Judah, right under Queen Athaliah's nose in the palace adjacent to the temple? (2 Kin. 11:4–8; 2 Chr. 23:1–7)

How was seven-year-old Joash crowned king of Judah? (2 Kin. 11:9–12; 2 Chr. 23:8–11)

What happened when Queen Athaliah became aware that her youngest grandson had survived and been crowned king in the temple next door to the palace? (2 Kin. 11:13–16; 2 Chr. 23:12–15)

What ceremonies and official actions marked the final stages of Joash's coronation and accession to the throne of Judah? (2 Kin. 11:17–21; 2 Chr. 23:16–21)

Joash was the short form of the name Jehoash (2 Kin. 12:1). Don't be surprised to see either form applied to this king. How did King Joash initially plan to repair the 124-year-old temple after the neglect of Jehoram, Ahaziah, and Athaliah? (2 Kin. 12:4, 5; 2 Chr. 24:4, 5)

When twenty-three years had passed, and the priests and Levites had not gathered the funds or repaired the temple, how did King Joash take matters into his own hands? (2 Kin. 12:6–15; 2 Chr. 24:6–13)

What was done with the money left from repair funds when the renovation was done and with the money from the trespass and sin offerings? (2 Kin. 12:16; 2 Chr. 24:14)

The high priest Jehoiada had protected the boy Joash until he could be crowned. He guided the early reforms of

King Joash. And he was married to the king's aunt (2 Chr. 22:11b). No wonder he was buried among the kings when he died at age 130 (2 Chr. 24:15, 16). What happened to the spiritual life of King Joash and the spiritual climate of Judah after the death of Jehoiada the high priest? (2 Chr. 24:17–19)

What happened when Jehoiada's son Zechariah brought a message from the Holy Spirit rebuking King Joash for leaving the path the high priest had guided him along before? (2 Chr. 24:20–22)

What troubles came to King Joash because he had turned away from the Lord and abused His prophets who tried to help him? (2 Kin. 12:17, 18; 2 Chr. 24:23–25a)

Describe the undignified end of King Joash, who began so well as a boy king under the guidance of Jehoiada the high priest. (2 Kin. 12:19–21; 2 Chr. 24:25b–27)

 FAITH ALIVE

What sorts of things happen in the hearts and minds of energetic, godly men and women who tire of godliness or lose their way as they grow older?

As you think about your own weaknesses and tendencies, what will you need to guard against to remain true to the Lord through all your days?

STRONG IN THE MIGHT OF THE FLESH

The descendants of Jehu proved strong rulers in the northern kingdom of Israel. By the time of Jeroboam II, Israel was a dominant power in the region. But the Lord was not impressed, and the Bible doesn't say much about Jeroboam. After all, the arm of flesh is not what matters in God's eyes.

What happened to King Jehoahaz, the first descendant of Jehu, because he "followed the sins of Jeroboam the son of Nebat" (2 Kin. 13:2) by leading Israel in worshiping the golden calves at Dan and Bethel? (2 Kin. 13:1–3)

What happened when King Jehoahaz of Israel cried out to the Lord for deliverance from the oppression of the Syrians? (2 Kin. 13:4, 5)

In what condition did King Jehoahaz leave the kingdom of Israel because he would not abandon idolatry? (2 Kin. 13:6, 7)

From reading 2 Kings 13:10–13, what impressions do you have of the reign of King Jehoash/Joash of the northern kingdom of Israel?

When King Amaziah of Judah wanted to do battle with King Joash of Israel, how did Joash answer him? What did that answer mean? (2 Kin. 13:12; 2 Chr. 25:17–19)

What was the outcome of King Joash's reluctant battle with Amaziah of Judah? (2 Chr. 25:20–24)

Elisha had ministered in the northern kingdom of Israel more than fifty years when he became fatally ill (2 Kin. 13:14).[2] How did ungodly King Joash react to news that the elderly prophet was dying? (2 Kin. 13:14)

How did the Lord direct Elisha to give a message of deliverance to King Joash? (2 Kin. 13:15–17)

How did King Joash of Israel show his lukewarm attitude toward the very encouraging message of the Lord through Elisha? (2 Kin. 13:18, 19)

How did the power of God that had marked Elisha's ministry during his life manifest itself even after his death? (2 Kin. 13:20, 21)

How did the Lord fulfill His prophecy of deliverance made through Elisha and limited by King Joash's halfhearted response? (2 Kin. 13:22–25)

 WORD WEALTH

Was gracious (2 Kin. 13:23) translates a Hebrew verb meaning "to have compassion on, to bestow favor on a person in need." **Was gracious,** as used in this context, denotes the kind of compassion, kindness, and consideration that will cause one to refrain from further wounding any bruised and suffering individual. God is very gracious, both by His own choice and by His very nature.[3]

What kind of king was Amaziah of Judah who began his reign during the second year of King Joash of Israel? (2 Kin. 14:1–6; 2 Chr. 25:1–4)

What was King Amaziah's great military success during his reign? (2 Kin. 14:7; 2 Chr. 25:5, 11, 12)

What valuable lesson did King Amaziah learn by rejecting the aid of the mercenaries from Israel when he battled the Edomites? (2 Chr. 25:6–10)

What unexpected spiritual defeat followed King Amaziah's faith-inspired military victory over the Edomites? (2 Chr. 25:14–16)

What act of pride and self-destruction followed King Amaziah's idolatry with the gods of Edom? (2 Chr. 25:17–24)

What were the consequences for the kingdom of Judah of King Amaziah's defeat and capture by King Joash of Israel? (2 Kin. 13:13, 14; 2 Chr. 25:23, 24)

King Amaziah was held captive by King Joash of Israel for some time, during which his son Azariah (Uzziah) acted as co-regent. When Amaziah was released and went home to Jerusalem, his presence probably muddied the political waters.[4] What kind of political confusion marked the final years of King Amaziah's life? (2 Kin. 14:17–20; 2 Chr. 25:25–28)

The third descendant of King Jehu to rule the northern kingdom of Israel was Jeroboam II. What was his reign like? (2 Kin. 14:23, 24)

What was the great accomplishment of King Jeroboam's reign? (2 Kin. 14:25)

Why did the Lord allow this ungodly king to expand Israel to roughly the borders of David's and Solomon's realms? (2 Kin. 14:26–28)

BEHIND THE SCENES

King Azariah/Uzziah of Judah was King Jeroboam II's contemporary. While Jeroboam II expanded Israel's borders, Azariah/Uzziah did the same for Judah. These two powerful kings between them approximated David's realm at its greatest extent. The tremendous difference between them was that Jeroboam II operated in the flesh and Azariah/Uzziah operated in the Spirit.

FAITH ALIVE

What do you think God wants unbelievers to realize when He allows them tremendous success in the course of their exercise of worldly power?

Why is it difficult for believers to watch unbelievers succeed and take all the credit for themselves?

How do you think God wants us to respond to the worldly success of unbelievers?

1. "You Snooze, You Lose," *Newsweek* (July 21, 1997), 50.
2. Richard D. Patterson and Hermann L. Austel, "1, 2 Kings," *The Expositor's Bible Commentary,* Vol. 4 (Grand Rapids: Zondervan Publishing House, 1988), 226.
3. *Spirit-Filled Life® Bible* (Nashville: Thomas Nelson Publishers, 1991), 1383, 1384, "Word Wealth, Mal. 1:9, be gracious."
4. Richard D. Patterson and Hermann L. Austel, "1, 2 Kings," *The Expositor's Bible Commentary,* Vol. 4, 229.

Lesson 9/ Reaping the Whirlwind

2 Kings 15—17;
2 Chronicles 26—28
(791—722 B.C.)

A man grew disenchanted with the rat race of urban life and decided to move to the country and become a chicken farmer. He bought a farmhouse, some acreage, and two hundred baby chicks. The chicks quickly died. He bought another two hundred, and just as rapidly they died too.

Puzzled and distressed, the rookie chicken farmer wrote his county agricultural agent and described in detail all his efforts to succeed in raising chickens. His letter ended, "I want very much to be a successful chicken farmer. Therefore, can you tell me: have I been planting the chicks too close together or too deep?"

The county agent answered by return post, "I can't answer your question until you send me a soil sample."

The adage says, "You reap what you sow," but some things aren't meant to be sown. God never meant poultry to be planted by ranchers or idolatry to be practiced by His people. Sow chicks and you destroy them; sow idolatry and you destroy your own soul. When God graciously blessed the reign of Jeroboam II (2 Kin. 14:25–27), no one responded to His grace. The day of reckoning for the northern kingdom of Israel then rushed to meet the ten northern tribes who never acted like they saw the end coming.

GLORY AND PRIDE IN JUDAH

Meanwhile in Judah, the third king in a row began well but gave way to the temptations of pride when he became successful and powerful. First Joash, then Amaziah, and now Azariah/Uzziah are credited by biblical writers with being good kings who had trouble ending as well as they started.

Summarize the basic facts about the reign of Azariah/Uzziah, king of Judah. (2 Kin. 15:1–4; 2 Chr. 26:1–5)

How did the Lord enable King Uzziah to prosper during the early years of his reign? (2 Chr. 26:6–10)

Describe the strength of the army and weapons of Judah under the command of King Uzziah. (2 Chr. 26:11–15)

 BEHIND THE SCENES

The reigns of Jeroboam II of Israel and Azariah/Uzziah of Judah overlapped by about forty years. During those decades Israel and Judah both expanded and prospered dramatically. In both kingdoms, prosperity led to spiritual lethargy. God challenged both with the ministries of several writing prophets. Toward the end of the era Isaiah prophesied in Judah. Joel, Amos, and Hosea warned Israel of impending doom. Obadiah and Jonah delivered divine oracles about or to the surrounding nations.[1]

How did Uzziah's pride about his accomplishments as king of Judah express itself? (2 Chr. 26:16–18)

What were the consequences of King Uzziah's pride? (2 Kin. 15:5–7; 2 Chr. 26:19–23)

BIBLE EXTRA

Read Isaiah 6:1–7. King Uzziah had done something unholy and unclean in the temple (2 Chr. 26:16–21). In the year Uzziah died, Isaiah had a vision of holiness and cleansing in the temple involving "the King, / The LORD of hosts" (Isa. 6:5). How many ways can you observe in which the glorious vision Isaiah witnessed contrasts with the outrage Uzziah committed?

FAITH ALIVE

Pride is Satan's own great sin. He understands it better than any other temptation. What do you think are the greatest dangers you face from the temptation of pride?

How has God worked in your life to reveal the dangers of pride? Who has he put close to you to tell you when you're out of line?

TREACHERY AND DECLINE IN ISRAEL

Three assassinations had marked a time of turmoil in the political life of Judah. Ahaziah (2 Kin. 9:27), Joash (12:20), and Amaziah (14:19) all died violently. But that was nothing compared to the carnage in the palace of the northern kingdom of Israel after the death of Jeroboam II. The end was drawing near.

The fourth descendant of Jehu son of Nimshi to rule over the northern kingdom of Israel was Zechariah. What was his reign like? (2 Kin. 15:8, 9)

What happened to King Zechariah of the northern kingdom of Israel? What does it mean that this could happen in public with no reported protest? (2 Kin. 15:10)

How did King Zechariah's death fulfill "the word of the LORD?" (2 Kin. 15:12; see 10:30)

Shallum, Zechariah's assassin, never achieved acceptance. In Assyrian records he was referred to contemptuously as "Shallum, son of nobody."[2] What became of King Shallum? (2 Kin. 15:13, 14)

How did Menahem assure that he would sit more securely on the throne of Israel than Shallum had? (2 Kin. 15:14, 16)

What was King Menahem's reign over the northern kingdom of Israel like? (2 Kin. 15:17, 18)

For fifty years the Assyrian empire had been troubled by internal rebellions and uprisings to the east. When Tiglath-Pileser (known as Pul in Babylon) became emperor, he settled those conflicts and turned his attention to the west.[3] How did King Menahem of Israel deal with the threat of the powerful Assyrian emperor? (2 Kin. 15:19, 20)

King Menahem managed to die a natural death and pass the throne of Israel on to his son Pekahiah (2 Kin. 15:22). What happened to King Pekahiah after he succeeded his father? (2 Kin. 15:23–26)

BEHIND THE SCENES

Pekah, who assassinated King Pekahiah, is said to have reigned twenty years (2 Kin. 15:27). But there were only eighteen years between the fifty-second year of Azariah/Uzziah of Judah when Pekah began his reign and 722 B.C. when Israel was destroyed by Assyria. King Hoshea's nine years have to fit in that time period too (17:1). Many scholars conclude that Pekah must have been a power in transjordanian Gilead for more than ten years before assassinating Pekahiah, and that he dated his reign from a time eleven years prior to taking the throne in Samaria.[4]

What was King Pekah's reign over the northern kingdom of Israel like? (2 Kin. 15:27, 28)

How did the Lord use King Pekah along with the king of Syria to punish King Ahaz and Judah? (2 Chr. 28:5–8)

How did King Pekah's army and its leaders respond to the message from the Lord through the prophet Oded about the treatment of fellow-Hebrew captives? (2 Chr. 28:5–15)

How did the Assyrian army under Tiglath-Pileser deal with King Pekah of Israel? (2 Kin. 15:29)

How did King Pekah's reign over the northern kingdom of Israel end? (2 Kin. 15:30)

ASSYRIAN CAMPAIGNS AGAINST ISRAEL AND JUDAH (734–732 B.C.)[5]

BEHIND THE SCENES

In the twenty-one years between 752 and 731 B.C., five kings ruled over the northern kingdom of Israel. Four of them died at assassins' hands. Shallum killed Zechariah. Menahem killed Shallum. Pekahiah succeeded his father Menahem and was murdered by Pekah. In turn Pekah met his death at Hoshea's hands.

When Jeroboam founded the kingdom of Israel, he instituted calf worship to stabilize and preserve the country. King Ahab married Jezebel to ally Israel with the powerful Phoenician forces of Sidon. In seeking worldly security both of those kings let loose in Israel the spiritual forces that led to the kind of godlessness, immorality, and violence that eventually tore Israel apart from within.

FAITH ALIVE

Why, when people start creating their own morality without reference to the living God, do they end up with systems that justify violence?

What do you think it says about the spiritual life of a Christian or a church when he, she, or it enjoys verbally assassinating the leaders God provides?

CLOSING THE TEMPLE IN JUDAH

While the northern kingdom of Israel disintegrated from internal violence and external pressures from Assyria, the southern kingdom of Judah also weakened after the glory days under King Azariah/Uzziah. Eventually Assyrian pressure would prompt a king of Judah to change public worship of the Lord to make it more "acceptable" to the pagan empire.

Describe the reign of King Jotham of the southern kingdom of Judah according to these points.

- General characteristics (2 Kin. 15:32–34; 2 Chr. 27:1, 2, 8)

- Greatest negative feature (2 Kin. 15:35)

- Greatest accomplishments (2 Chr. 27:3–6)

- Most ominous development (2 Kin. 15:37)

What was the reign of Jotham's son Ahaz like in the southern kingdom of Judah? (2 Kin. 16:1–4; 2 Chr. 28:1–4)

BEHIND THE SCENES

King Solomon had sacrificed and burnt incense to idols in pagan temples and on high places (1 Kin. 11:5–8). Kings Jehoram and Ahaziah of Judah, under the influence of Athaliah, their wife and mother respectively, imitated the religious practices of King Ahab and Queen Jezebel of Israel (2 Kin. 8:18, 27). But King Ahaz was the first to go so far as to practice infant sacrifice (16:3). He would not be the last (21:6).

What was the greatest military threat King Ahaz faced as he tried to govern the southern kingdom of Judah? (2 Kin. 16:5)

Although the Syrian-Israelite coalition was unable to capture Jerusalem (2 Kin. 16:5), how much damage did it inflict on Judah? (2 Chr. 28:5–8)

What former subject peoples took advantage of King Ahaz's difficulties with Syria and Israel to rebel against Judah and expand at her expense? (2 Kin. 16:6; 2 Chr. 28:17, 18)

How did King Ahaz try to save Judah from the troubles that surrounded it? (2 Kin. 16:7, 8; 2 Chr. 28:16, 21)

BIBLE EXTRA

The Lord directed the prophet Isaiah to proclaim to King Ahaz that Israel and Syria would not defeat Judah if Judah would rely on Him for deliverance (Is. 7:1–9). The prophet challenged King Ahaz to ask for a sign from God validating this prophecy, but the king said he would not dare test God (vv. 10–12). Isaiah gave King Ahaz a sign anyway. "Behold, the virgin shall conceive and bear a Son, and shall call His name Immanuel" (v. 14). Before that child would know right from wrong both Syria and Israel's kings would be gone (v. 16). Of course, that prophecy had a second, deeper significance that expressed itself in Bethlehem more than seven hundred years later and continues to speak 2,700 years later to a lost world.

How did King Ahaz's appeal to Assyria for help against Syria and Israel turn out?

- In terms of removing immediate pressure (2 Kin. 16:9)

- In terms of freeing Judah from external pressure over the long term (2 Chr. 28:20, 21)

 KINGDOM EXTRA

Holiness requires that we guard our associations. Avoid the evil ethic of expediency. Do not employ procedures or practices you suspect are unethical or ungodly, even if they promise success.[6]

How did King Ahaz's contacts with pagan rulers cause him to modify the temple in Jerusalem? Why did he do this? (2 Kin. 16:10–16; 2 Chr. 28:28)

What changes in the temple furnishings did King Ahaz make in order to have some valuable metals on hand for further tribute payments and national operating expenses? (2 Kin. 16:17, 18; see 1 Kin. 7:23–39)

As this process continued, what was the eventual result of King Ahaz's desecration of the temple of the Lord in Jerusalem? (2 Chr. 28:24, 25)

How did the officials and people of Judah react to the death of King Ahaz? (2 Chr. 28:27)

 ### FAITH ALIVE

What are some of the pressures of life and the world that tend to create panic in your heart and fear that the Lord may not be able to handle them?

God often works through human agents to accomplish His purposes. But our confidence always should be on the Lord rather than His instrument. At times like those listed in the previous question, our focus will shift from trusting God to trusting something or someone else. When panic has distorted your faith, who or what do you tend to rely on rather than God?

What promises of God's Word do you need to ask the Holy Spirit to keep sounding in your soul so you don't shut down the temple of your heart in times of distress?

ISRAEL REMOVED AND REPLACED

In fulfillment of Isaiah's prophecy (Is. 7:1, 4–9, 14–16), King Pekah of Israel was shortly assassinated and replaced by the man who would be the last king of the northern kingdom. By the time King Ahaz himself died, Israel had ceased to exist.

How is the reign of Hoshea, Israel's final king, characterized? (2 Kin. 17:1, 2)

Tiglath-Pileser, emperor of Assyria, had by Hoshea's time been succeeded by his son Shalmaneser. How did King

Hoshea handle his relations with the Assyrian Empire as his reign unfolded? (2 Kin. 17:3, 4)

In a surprisingly brief statement, the biblical text records the fate of King Hoshea, Samaria, the capital city of Israel, and the population of Israel. What happened to them? (2 Kin. 17:4–6)

1. King Hoshea

2. Samaria, the capital of Israel

3. The Israelite population

ASSYRIAN CAMPAIGNS AGAINST ISRAEL[7]

WORD WEALTH

Provoke to anger (2 Kin. 17:11) translates a Hebrew verb that means to grieve, exasperate, vex, provoke, or make angry. This word portrays the kind of anger that results from repeated provocation, and not the anger that suddenly explodes at the first offense. It is closer to "exasperation" than to "wrath."[8] The patience of God causes Him to put up with so much provocation; the justice of God requires that He finally respond with judgment.

How had Israel sinned in each of these ways and so compelled the Lord to judge them by means of the Assyrians?

* Through idolatry (2 Kin. 17:7–12)

* Through ignoring His warnings (2 Kin. 17:13, 14)

* Through breaking their covenant with Him (2 Kin. 17:15, 17)

KINGDOM EXTRA

Unholiness dishonors God. Understand that God judges His people severely when they persist in the world's ways and standards rather than His. Reject any areas where worldly-mindedness has taken root in you.[9]

What warning should the remaining tribe of Judah (along with the portions of Benjamin, Levi, and other tribes associated with the southern kingdom) have learned from the fate of Israel? (2 Kin. 17:18, 19)

What was the sin of Israel that symbolized or summed up all the others in the eyes of God? (2 Kin. 17:20–23)

The Assyrians replaced the deported population of Israel with people displaced by other wars from their homelands throughout Mesopotamia (2 Kin. 17:24). How did these immigrants learn the distorted worship of the Lord that had been practiced in Israel since the days of Jeroboam? (2 Kin. 17:25–28)

What did the immigrants into Israel from Mesopotamia do with the religious instruction they received from the priest at Bethel? (2 Kin. 17:29–33)

What was wrong with the practice of the Mesopotamian immigrant of worshiping the Lord and their native gods? (2 Kin. 17:34–40)

1. Richard D. Patterson and Hermann L. Austel, "1, 2 Kings," *The Expositor's Bible Commentary,* Vol. 4 (Grand Rapids: Zondervan Publishing House, 1988), 233.
2. Dilday, Russell, *Mastering the Old Testament,* Volume 9, 1, 2 Kings (Dallas: Word Publishing, 1987), 403.
3. "1, 2 Kings," *The Expositor's Bible Commentary,* Vol. 4, 237.
4. Ibid., 238, 239.
5. *Spirit-Filled Life® Bible* (Nashville: Thomas Nelson Publishers, 1991), 551, map "Assyrian Campaigns Against Israel and Judah (734–732 B.C.).
6. Ibid., 654, "Truth-in-Action through 2 Chronicles."
7. Ibid., 554, map "Assyrian Campaigns Against Israel (725 B.C.)."
8. Ibid., 512, "Word Wealth, 1 Kin. 16:2, anger."
9. Ibid., 569, "Truth-in-Action through 2 Kings."

Lesson 10/Glory Before Nightfall
2 Kings 18—20;
2 Chronicles 29—32
(729—699 B.C.)

Herodotus, the Greek historian, narrated a story about the pharaoh of Egypt contemporary with King Hezekiah of Judah. Herodotus called the pharaoh Sethos. Sethos was a priest and he neglected the warrior class of Egypt to the point that they would not defend him when the Assyrians threatened to invade the delta country.

Sethos claimed that a god came to him in a dream and encouraged him to go face Sennacherib and the Assyrian army without the trained soldiers of Egypt. Accordingly, Sethos led a motley collection of merchants, craftsmen, and laborers to the Egyptian frontier where they pitched camp and waited for the Assyrians. They came and set up camp facing the Egyptians.

The story goes that in the night before the battle, mice overran the Assyrian camp and ate everything leather. The next morning no bows had strings, no arrows had quivers, no swords had sheaths, and no shields had handles. The highly-trained Assyrians were effectively unarmed, fell before the amateur troops of Egypt, and broke into a rout.[1]

Herodotus's story, whether based on fact or totally legendary, pales before what really happened when the same Sennacherib later tried to capture Jerusalem against the Lord God of Israel's wishes. King Hezekiah epitomized the kind of godly king the Lord wanted to reign over His people. The blessing that Hezekiah enjoyed even as judgment fell on the northern kingdom of Israel reveals the glory God wants to pour out on those who love and serve Him.

THE GLORIOUS REVIVAL OF HEZEKIAH

King Hezekiah approached his reign as though he needed to reverse all of the evil policies and practices of his father King Ahaz. Efforts to coordinate the biblical numbers concerning the reigns of the kings of Israel and Judah suggest that Hezekiah reigned for a time alongside Ahaz, with the result that Ahaz was still alive when Assyria captured Samaria in 722 B.C., but Hezekiah was on the throne. That was all to Judah's benefit, because Hezekiah was a man with a mission.

King Hezekiah received the most positive evaluation of all the kings mentioned in 1 and 2 Kings. How did he merit this praise? (2 Kin. 18:1–6; 2 Chr. 29:1, 2; 32:27–29)

How is it possible for relics of great spiritual moments in the past, such as the bronze serpent Moses made (Num. 21:5–9), to become hindrances to true faith in God today? (see 2 Kin. 18:4)

Hezekiah's father Ahaz had closed the temple of the Lord in favor of worshiping the gods of neighboring countries (2 Chr. 17:22–25). How did Hezekiah go about reversing his father's evil policies? (2 Chr. 29:3–19)

What role did each of these components play in King Hezekiah's dedication ceremony of the cleansed temple of the Lord in Jerusalem?

- Sin offerings (2 Chr. 29:20–24)

- Music of praise (2 Chr. 29:25–30)

- Worship offerings (2 Chr. 29:31–36)

What were some of the unusual features of the Passover celebration King Hezekiah proposed some time after the temple worship was restored? (2 Chr. 30:1–5; see Num. 9:10, 11)

BEHIND THE SCENES

When the Assyrian armies deported the population of the ten northern tribes of Israel and resettled them in various parts of Mesopotamia, they removed the upper layers of a class-oriented society. The peasantry remained on the land in a disorganized condition, while the upper classes of other conquered people were moved in among them by the Assyrians. Somewhere in the first ten years after the northern kingdom fell to Assyria, King Hezekiah appealed to the peasants of Israel to return to the true worship of God at the temple in Jerusalem by joining in the Passover celebration.

How did King Hezekiah encourage inhabitants of Israel to celebrate the Passover in Jerusalem, and how did Israel respond? (2 Chr. 30:6–11)

How did the priests and Levites officiating over King Hezekiah's Passover respond to the special needs for purification of each of these groups?

- The worshipers from Judah (2 Chr. 30:13–16)

- The worshipers from Israel (2 Chr. 30:17–20)

KINGDOM EXTRA

Although many Israelites observing Passover had not prepared themselves properly according to sanctuary purification rites, Hezekiah's prayer entreated the Lord for His atonement on behalf of all who sought Him with pure hearts. Despite their failure to observe proper order in worship, the Lord was pleased with the attitude of their hearts, and He heard and healed. Reconciliation with God is the greatest healing miracle of all. God desires to mend the broken and estranged relationship with His people.[2]

How did the joy, praise, and worship of King Hezekiah's Passover unite the worshipers to one another and to the Lord? (2 Chr. 30:21–27)

WORD WEALTH

Assembly (2 Chr. 30:23) translates a Hebrew noun indicating a multitude that has been called together, a congregation. Roughly thirty times in Exodus through Deuteronomy **assembly** refers to the congregation of Israel traveling or camping in the wilderness. While the people comprised an actual family or nation, they were also a spiritual congregation. **Assembly** parallels the New Testament term "church."[3] The reunited **assembly** of Judah and Israel marked a spiritual high point when God's people were together for worship and personal, spiritual renewal.

How did Hezekiah's Passover lead Israel and Judah to express their love of God and one another in these ways?

1. Rejection of false gods and the occult (2 Chr. 31:1)

2. Support of God-ordained spiritual leaders (2 Chr. 31:2–19)

The writer of 2 Kings focused on the political and military aspects of King Hezekiah's reign. The chronicler chose to emphasize the spiritual reforms that Hezekiah made his priority from the first month of his rule (2 Chr. 29:3). Why were Hezekiah's spiritual reforms foundational to everything else he did? (2 Chr. 31:20, 21)

 FAITH ALIVE

What is the most powerful spiritual revival you have witnessed in a church or school or camp?

How did the Spirit of God work through leaders, praise, repentance, and purification to create that revival?

ATTACKED BY A SUPERPOWER

King Hezekiah had shown that he desired to please the Lord more than anything else in his life. Perhaps the most difficult test of this desire came as the prophet Isaiah repeatedly encouraged him to reject alliances with Assyria or Egypt (for example, Is. 31). Before Assyria conquered the northern kingdom of Israel, King Ahaz had aligned Judah with the Assyrians (2 Kin. 16:7–9).

How did King Hezekiah respond to the Assyrians and other traditional opponents of Judah? (2 Kin. 18:7, 8)

How did King Hezekiah prepare Jerusalem and Judah for the attack by the Assyrians that he knew would eventually come? (2 Chr. 32:2–8, 30)

What events forced King Hezekiah to reevaluate his policy of non-cooperation with the Assyrians? (2 Kin. 18:9–13; 2 Chr. 32:1)

What steps was King Hezekiah forced to take in response to the invasion of southern Judah by the Assyrian armies on their way back from defeating the Egyptians? (2 Kin. 18:14–16)

What did the officials of Assyria whom Sennacherib sent to Jerusalem along with a sizable contingent of troops have to say to Hezekiah's officials about Hezekiah's preparations to resist them? (2 Kin. 18:17–25; 2 Chr. 32:9–15)

When asked by Hezekiah's officials to conduct their negotiations in Aramaic rather than Hebrew, what appeals did the Assyrian officials make directly to the defenders of Jerusalem who could hear the diplomatic exchange? (2 Kin. 18:26–35; 2 Chr. 32:18, 19)

What mistaken ideas about the Lord God of Israel did the Assyrian diplomats base their assertions and predictions on? (2 Kin. 18:19–35)

What were the reactions of the common people and the officials of Judah to the propaganda, threats, and promises of the Assyrian delegation? (2 Kin. 18:36, 37)

How else did King Sennacherib of Assyria try to undermine the morale of Jerusalem and Judah? (2 Chr. 32:16, 17)

DELIVERED THROUGH THE ZEAL OF THE LORD

King Hezekiah and the residents of Jerusalem could antic-
ipate months of siege warfare with its accompanying starvation
and epidemic diseases. In the end they could expect to be tor-
tured and slaughtered in ways that amused their conquerors.
Terror would have been an understandable and excusable first
response on King Hezekiah's part to news of the threats of the
Assyrian delegation.

Instead of quaking with fear, how did King Hezekiah first
respond to the intimidation of the Assyrian ambassadors?
(2 Kin. 19:1–4)

 WORD WEALTH

The **prayer** (2 Kin. 19:4) King Hezekiah asked Isaiah to
make on behalf of the remnant left after Sennacherib's capture of the fortified cities of Judah was intercession toward the
temple in keeping with the kind of prayer Solomon had urged
(1 Kin. 8:30). This Hebrew noun occurs seventy-six times in
the Old Testament, thirty-two times alone in the Psalms. But
its other concentration is in 1 Kings 8 and 2 Chronicles 6
where fully thirty appearances of this noun and the verb it's
based on identify intercession toward the temple where God
focused His attention and presence in some way as a major
part of Old Testament spiritual warfare.[4]

What was Isaiah's prophetic word about the Lord's
response to the spiritual warfare Sennacherib and the Assyrians
had started by equating Him with the gods of the nations?
(2 Kin. 19:5–7)

How did the Assyrians keep the spiritual war going when
they had to abandon their planned attack on Hezekiah and
Jerusalem in order to deal with an uprising in Egypt under the
leadership of an Ethiopian military leader? (2 Kin. 19:8–13)

How did King Hezekiah respond to the further threats and blasphemies of the Assyrians as they withdrew temporarily from Judah to deal with Tirhakah and his army in Egypt? (2 Kin. 19:14–19)

 KINGDOM EXTRA

When King Hezekiah spread out Sennacherib's letter before the Lord in the temple, his physical action became prophetically symbolic of a spiritual reality. God granted the king authority in the spiritual realm based on his act of faith in the physical realm. Other physical acts in the Bible that played a role in creating spiritual authority include vocal praise and shouting (1 Sam. 4:5, 6; 1 Kin. 1:40), lifting hands and bowing heads (Neh. 8:6), dancing and leaping (Ps. 149:3; Luke 6:23), groaning in prayer (Rom. 8:26; Gal. 4:19), shaking or trembling (Acts 16:29; Heb. 12:21), intense weeping (Ezra 3:13; Lam. 1:16, 20), and many instances of prostration (Ezek. 1:26–28; Matt. 17:6; Acts 9:1–9; 10:9–14). Prompted by faith and prayer-passion, these can address the unseen as real—and gain victories.[5]

What did the Lord have to say to King Hezekiah through His spokesman, the prophet Isaiah, about each of these topics?

- The blasphemy of the Assyrians (2 Kin. 19:20–28)

- The future of the residents of Jerusalem (2 Kin. 19:29–31)

- Sennacherib, the Assyrian emperor (2 Kin. 19:32–34)

WORD WEALTH

Virgin (2 Kin. 19:21) represents a Hebrew noun denoting the physical chastity of an unmarried young woman. In combination with the name of a city or nation, **virgin** denotes the seat of beauty, virtue, and fruitfulness for that community. In this passage, the Lord implied that Sennacherib would never violate Jerusalem as long as she was under the watchful care of the Lord.[6] When Isaiah prophesied of the virgin mother of Immanuel (Is. 7:14), he used a different noun that suggested the young woman was ripe for marriage and childbirth.[7]

How did the Lord finalize the defeat of the massive Assyrian army which had won battle after battle between Nineveh and Egypt in order to protect Jerusalem and King Hezekiah? (2 Kin. 19:35–37; 2 Chr. 32:20–23)

THE INGLORIOUS PRIDE OF HEZEKIAH

Perhaps it saddens you to realize that even a man with the spiritual maturity of Hezekiah stumbled badly because of pride. Take heart, however. The writer of 2 Kings arranged his material topically. The events of 2 Kings 20 actually preceded those of chapter 19. Chronologically, Hezekiah recovered from his greatest failure to enjoy his greatest success.

What was King Hezekiah's reaction to the Word of the Lord, delivered by Isaiah the prophet, that he was going to die of his serious illness? (2 Kin. 20:1–3)

What was the Lord's reaction to Hezekiah's tearful prayers for healing from his fatal disease? (2 Kin. 20:4–7)

Hezekiah's father, King Ahaz, had refused to ask the Lord for a sign to validate His prophecy (Is. 7:10–13). Hezekiah did not hesitate to ask for confirmation of the Lord's Word. How did the Lord prove His message to Hezekiah? (2 Kin. 20:8–11)

KINGDOM EXTRA

God is the Author of all healing benefit. When He directed Isaiah to advise the application of a poultice of figs to King Hezekiah's ulcerous sore, He implied that human medical aid is always appropriate as an adjunct to His activity. God alone can heal: He does so by miraculous means, by natural means, and by man-made means. None should be demeaned as godless. As this text shows, deliverance from death comes from God no matter what means or agents He employs.[8]

Merodach Baladan (see Is. 39:1 for the correct form of his name) was trying to put together an alliance to oppose Assyria. This visit probably led to Hezekiah's decision to break with that empire (2 Kin. 18:7). Fifteen years before Hezekiah's death dates to about 712 B.C., nearly a dozen years before Sennacherib's advance on Jerusalem in 701 B.C. What occurred when the Babylonian envoys visited with Hezekiah? (2 Kin. 20:12, 13; 2 Chr. 32:31)

How did the prophet Isaiah interpret the events of the Babylonian visit to King Hezekiah? (2 Kin. 20:14–18)

How did King Hezekiah respond to the rebuke of the Lord through the prophet Isaiah? (2 Kin. 20:19; 2 Chr. 32:25, 26)

How did the nation of Judah react to the death of King Hezekiah? (2 Chr. 32:33)

FAITH ALIVE

King Hezekiah's pride sprang from the fact that God had miraculously healed him. How can our greatest spiritual blessings or victories become sources of temptation to prideful thoughts, words, and actions?

When our pride has been exposed and criticized, what are some fleshly reactions and some godly reactions we can make?

1. Herodotus, *The History*, II, 141.

2. *Hayford's Bible Handbook* (Nashville: Thomas Nelson Publishers, 1995), 108, note on 2 Chr. 30:18–20.

3. *Spirit-Filled Life® Bible* (Nashville: Thomas Nelson Publishers, 1991), 168, "Word Wealth, Lev. 16:17, assembly."

4. *Theological Wordbook of the Old Testament,* Vol. 2 (Chicago: Moody Press, 1980), 725, 726.

5. *Spirit-Filled Life® Bible*, 559, "Kingdom Dynamics, 2 Kin. 19:8–19, Physical Acts in Warfare Prayer."

6. Richard D. Patterson and Hermann L. Austel, "1, 2 Kings," *The Expositor's Bible Commentary*, Vol. 4 (Grand Rapids: Zondervan Publishing House, 1988), 267.

7. Geoffrey W. Grogan, "Isaiah," *The Expositor's Bible Commentary*, Vol. 6 (Grand Rapids: Zondervan Publishing House, 1988), 65.

8. *Spirit-Filled Life® Bible*, 560, 561, "Kingdom Dynamics, 2 Kin. 20:1–11, Healing by Miracle or Medicine?"

Lesson 11/The Worst of Times; the Best of Times

2 Kings 21:1—23:30;
2 Chronicles 33—35
(698—609 B.C.)

Charles Dickens began *A Tale of Two Cities* with the line "It was the best of times, it was the worst of times." London and Paris during the era of the French Revolution provided the setting and circumstances that revealed the noblest and ignoblest qualities in the hearts of characters in the novel. The reader closes the volume with a sense that good has triumphed over evil.

As 2 Kings and 2 Chronicles draw to their respective closes, two kings dominate the stage as the future of God's relationship with the southern kingdom of Judah hangs in the balance. The first is Judah's most wicked king; the second is the one most devoted to the Word of God. But when you close the book on the best king's life, your heart is heavy with a sense of doom. Evil is so deeply rooted in the hearts of the people of Judah that it will take judgment to do what godly leadership and inspired prophets have failed to accomplish—root it out.

It was the worst of times, and not even the best of revivals could do more than postpone the storm whose clouds darkened the horizon.

BAD AS THEY COULD BE

The spiritual pendulum was swinging in the lineup of kings of Judah. Ahaz introduced child sacrifice and closed the temple of the Lord. Then Hezekiah refurbished the temple, removed pagan shrines, and set a new standard for trust in the Lord during national emergencies. Hezekiah's son determined to model himself after his grandfather rather than his father.

What were some of the things that King Manasseh did to establish his reputation as Judah's most evil king? (2 Kin. 21:1–6; 2 Chr. 33:1–6)

What evil practices did Manasseh pursue that the earlier wicked kings had not? (2 Kin. 21:3–6; compare 1 Kin. 16:30–33; 2 Kin. 16:3, 4)

What sin of King Manasseh did the biblical writers single out as being especially wicked? Why was it so serious? (2 Kin. 21:7–9; 2 Chr. 33:7–9)

     ## BIBLE EXTRA

The pagan and occult practices King Manasseh introduced or reintroduced into the spiritual life of Judah were forbidden in the Law of Moses. The leaders of Judah had to be ignorant of or indifferent to the Law to allow these things to happen. Subsequent events suggest the Law had been neglected so long people were ignorant of its demands (2 Kin. 22:10–13).

Worship on the high places violated God's command that His people worship at the central sanctuary He provided them (Deut. 12:2–7). Image-making and idolatry violated the Ten Commandments (Ex. 20:3–6; Deut. 5:7–10). Worshiping the sun, moon, planets, and stars conformed to the Assyrian and Babylonian fascination with astrology, but it violated Moses' express prohibition of such worship as a particularly vile form of idolatry worthy of death (Deut. 4:19; 17:2–5).

Child sacrifice, fortune-telling, witchcraft, necromancy, and spiritism all violated the Law of God and moved the king and His people closer and closer to Satan's realm and farther and farther from the rule of the Lord (Lev. 18:21; 20:2; Deut.

18:10–14). Judah was becoming a culture of death because of its fascination with all that is hellish. No society should knowingly follow her down that path.

What judicial sentence did the Lord pronounce on Judah because of the sin of Manasseh? (2 Kin. 21:10–15)

What shade of meaning does each of these metaphors add to the description of the judgment facing Judah because of her sins during the reign of Manasseh? (2 Kin. 21:12, 13)

• Tingling ears

• The measuring line or plumb line

• The wiped dish

What other sinful pattern by King Manasseh led to judgment on the southern kingdom of Judah? (2 Kin. 21:16)

What personal judgment fell on King Manasseh about six years before the end of his fifty-five-year reign, and what was its outcome? (2 Chr. 33:10–13)

What additional information about Manasseh was available to the original readers of 2 Kings and 2 Chronicles? (2 Kin. 21:17; 2 Chr. 33:18, 19)

How did King Amon's brief reign turn out following his father Manasseh's late-in-life repentance and renewal? (2 Kin. 21:19–22; 2 Chr. 33:21–23)

What bloody actions marked the end of King Amon's brief reign? (2 Kin. 21:23, 24; 2 Chr. 33:24, 25)

FAITH ALIVE

What immoral, idolatrous, and devilish contemporary practices should give Christians cause for concern about the rise of a culture of death that threatens the future of our society?

What weapons of spiritual warfare should we employ to combat the effects of the devil's culture of death?

How do you think Christians are to act as salt and light (Matt. 5:13–16) in a decadent society?

REDISCOVERING THE WORD OF GOD

No matter how spiritually dark and hopeless a situation may seem, God can shine His light into it. Manasseh and Amon introduced terrible paganism and occultism into Judah. Then God raised up the greatest reformer of Judah's history. Hezekiah exhibited the greatest faith in the Lord of Judah's kings; his great grandson Josiah exhibited the greatest commitment to the Word of the Lord.

What were the high points of each of these four years in King Josiah's life?

- Eight years old (2 Kin. 22:1; 2 Chr. 34:1)

- Sixteen years old (2 Chr. 34:3)

- Twenty years old (2 Chr. 34:3–7)

- Twenty-six years old (2 Kin. 22:3–8; 23:3; 2 Chr. 35:18, 19)

BEHIND THE SCENES

By the time of Josiah's reign, Assyrian power in Palestine was effectively over, but Babylonian might had not reached so far yet. King Hezekiah had been able to exert some influence over the former territory of the northern kingdom of Israel (2 Chr. 30:5–11), but King Josiah could take direct action and compel the people living in Israel to obey him (2 Kin. 23:15–20; 2 Chr. 34:6, 7). For a brief time, Josiah exercised a measure of dominion over the realm David and Solomon had ruled.

In the eighteenth year of his reign, how did King Josiah see that needed repairs were carried out on the temple? (2 Kin. 22:3–7; 2 Chr. 34:8–13)

What totally unexpected event occurred while Hilkiah the high priest was getting the temple ready for repairs? (2 Kin. 22:8; 2 Chr. 34:14, 15)

How did Shaphan the royal recorder handle the discovery of the Law in the temple? (2 Kin. 22:9, 10; 2 Chr. 34:16–18)

What was King Josiah's reaction to hearing the long-neglected and forgotten Law of God? (2 Kin. 22:11–13; 2 Chr. 34:19–21)

What message did the Lord send King Josiah through Huldah the prophetess? (2 Kin. 22:14–20; 2 Chr. 34:22–28)

How do you imagine King Josiah felt when the Lord told him his repentance and revival would defer judgment during his lifetime but would not prevent it from coming? (2 Kin. 22:16–20; 2 Chr. 34:24–28)

 WORD WEALTH

Provoke to anger (2 Chr. 34:25) translates a Hebrew verb that means to grieve, exasperate, vex, provoke, or make angry. This word portrays the kind of anger that results from repeated provocation, not the anger that suddenly explodes at the first offense. It is closer to "exasperation" than to "wrath."[1] Such provocation had caused the Lord to send the northern kingdom of Israel into exile (2 Kin. 17:11). Now it was bringing His judgment on Judah as well.

 FAITH ALIVE

When has the Word of God convicted you of sin to the point that you were moved to tears of sorrow?

What impact does it have when you see an unfamiliar passage of Scripture that really applies to you?

What godly woman leader has had the most profound spiritual impact on your life through her ministry? What made her such an effective servant of God?

THE GLORIOUS REFORMER

Clearly the most important event of Josiah's reign occurred in its eighteenth year, when the Law of God was discovered in the temple while it was being refurbished. The discovery of the Law was accompanied by a flurry of spiritual reforms and celebrations that must have occurred simultaneously because they all apparently took place within that same eighteenth regnal year.

What two-step process did King Josiah initiate to let the people of Judah know about the Book of the Covenant which Hilkiah the priest had found in the temple?

1. (2 Kin. 23:1, 2; 2 Chr. 34:29, 30)

2. (2 Kin. 23:3; 2 Chr. 34:31, 32)

 BEHIND THE SCENES

"The Book of the Covenant" (2 Kin. 23:2, 21) is a synonym for "the Book of the Law" (22:8) found by Hilkiah the priest in the temple. Just how much of the Law of Moses was included in this book is uncertain. The Book of the Covenant may have been all of the Pentateuch or, more likely, Deuteronomy.[2] It could have been portions of the Law which stress the covenant between God and His people, such as Exodus 20—23, Leviticus 26; Deuteronomy 27—30).[3]

Once King Josiah and the people had obligated themselves to keep the Law, what spiritual reforms did Josiah carry out in the villages and towns throughout Judah? (2 Kin. 23:8, 9)

What evil practices of Manasseh and other kings of Judah did Josiah root out in Jerusalem? (2 Kin. 23:10–12)

What 300-year-old practices dating back to Solomon (1 Kin. 11:7, 8) did King Josiah end in his reforms? (2 Kin. 23:13, 14)

How did Josiah deal with King Jeroboam's center of idolatry at Bethel (1 Kin. 12:28–33), which had started the northern kingdom of Israel's long slide away from the Lord? (2 Kin. 23:15–20)

As part of his thorough reform of the official worship of the Lord in Judah, King Josiah ordered the observance of a glorious Passover in the eighteenth year of his reign. King Hezekiah also had conducted a Passover observance during his reforms (2 Chr. 30). Hezekiah's Passover had been spontaneous and slightly makeshift; Josiah's was carefully planned by the Book. How does the Bible characterize King Josiah's Passover celebration? (2 Kin. 23:21–23; 2 Chr. 35:18, 19)

What instructions did King Josiah give to the priests and Levites who would assist the Passover worshipers? (2 Chr. 35:1–6)

What elements made up King Josiah's celebration on that Passover day in preparation for the week-long Feast of Unleavened Bread? (2 Chr. 35:10–17)

In 609 B.C., Pharaoh Necho of Egypt marched his army north along the Mediterranean coast toward Carchemish on the upper Euphrates River to assist the weakening Assyrian army resist the forces of a newly assertive Babylon.[4] Josiah wanted Assyria and Egypt weak and evidently did not foresee trouble from Babylon. What was the outcome of King Josiah's confrontation with Pharaoh Necho at Megiddo? (2 Kin. 23:29; 2 Chr. 35:20–23)

What was the reaction of the kingdom of Judah to King Josiah's death in battle? (2 Kin. 23:30; 2 Chr. 35:24, 25)

What was King Josiah's biblical epitaph? (2 Kin. 23:24, 25)

 FAITH ALIVE

As the Holy Spirit of God has purified your life to conform you to the image of Christ, what worldly habits and patterns of thought is He stripping away from you?

What has been your most incredible worship experience? What made it so profound?

1. *Spirit-Filled Life® Bible* (Nashville: Thomas Nelson Publishers, 1991), 512, "Word Wealth, 1 Kin. 16:2, anger."

2. J. Barton Payne, "1, 2 Chronicles," *The Expositor's Bible Commentary,* Vol. 4 (Grand Rapids: Zondervan Publishing House, 1988), 551.

3. Richard D. Patterson and Hermann L. Austel, "1, 2 Kings," *The Expositor's Bible Commentary,* Vol. 4, 287.

4. Donald J. Wiseman, *1 and 2 Kings: An Introduction and Commentary* (Leicester, England: InterVarsity Press, 1993), 305.

Lesson 12/The Glory Has Departed

2 Kings 23:31—25:30;
2 Chronicles 36
(609—586 B.C.)

"Elvis has left the building," they used to say to indicate that "The King" was gone for the night. His presence no longer animated the place. And Elvis did have an aura his fans felt and responded to. At first, his charisma made him larger than life. Later it was his image, propped up by hype and fan devotion.

Then Elvis Presley died. Faced with the prospect of living without their hero, many refused to let go of him. Tabloid writers gladly feed the appetites of "true believers" for "evidence" that The King is still alive. In death, Elvis has become an industry.

The alternative is to admit that Elvis's glory has departed; maybe to face the possibility that the glory had faded pretty badly before he died. Deny reality long enough and it gets harder and harder to face it.

As the seventh century B.C. ended and the sixth began, the residents of Judah and Jerusalem faced a much more serious dilemma. King Josiah had died after the greatest spiritual reforms of Judah's history. Could the prophet Jeremiah be right that the end was near because of their persistent disobedience? Could the glory depart so soon? Almost everybody denied the possibility.

PUPPETS OF EGYPT AND BABYLON

After Pharaoh Necho's forces defeated King Josiah's army and killed the king at Megiddo (2 Kin. 23:29), Judah entered a humiliating period when foreign powers dictated who would be king. The foreign powers respected the legitimacy of the Davidic dynasty, but they showed their control by choosing the name under which each king would rule.

What happened to Josiah's son Jehoahaz, who succeeded his father after his death in battle against Pharaoh Necho? (2 Kin. 23:31–34; 2 Chr. 36:3, 4)

BIBLE EXTRA

What had been Jehoahaz's personal name before he became king? (Jer. 22:11) Was he Josiah's firstborn son? (1 Chr. 3:15)

In the genealogy recorded in 1 Chronicles 3:15, Shallum/Jehoahaz is listed fourth. The first son, Johanan, may have died young since he isn't mentioned again. Jehoiakim and Zedekiah are grouped second and third because they each had long reigns. Shallum, who reigned but three months at age twenty-three, actually was older than Zedekiah, who would have been about ten years old when Shallum/Jehoahaz was king.

How did Pharaoh Necho demonstrate Egyptian domination of the kingdom of Judah? (2 Kin. 23:33–35; 2 Chr. 36:4)

Describe the reign of Josiah's younger son Eliakim/Jehoiakim. (2 Kin. 24:35–37; 2 Chr. 36:5)

How did the international political situation change for Judah and King Jehoiakim during his eleven-year reign? (2 Kin. 24:1, 7)

How did the Lord initially chastise King Jehoiakim for his wicked ways? (2 Kin. 24:2–4)

BEHIND THE SCENES

The prophet Jeremiah described King Jehoiakim as an aggressively evil king. He lived in luxury (Jer. 22:14, 15) while oppressing the poor (vv. 13, 17). He persecuted any prophet who dared deliver a word from the Lord against him (26:21–24; 32:36). Jehoiakim's most blatant rejection of God's will occurred when he cut up the scroll of Jeremiah's prophecies and burned the fragments in the charcoal brazier that heated his winter quarters (36:22, 23).

In 605 B.C., Nebuchadnezzar of Babylon came to Jerusalem to rebuke Jehoiakim for rebelling against him. How did Nebuchadnezzar punish Jehoiakim? (2 Chr. 36:6, 7)

When Jehoiakim died and his son Jehoiachin became king, the Babylonian army was once more on its way to Judah because Jehoiakim had again broken his treaty with Nebuchadnezzar. What was the result for eighteen-year-old Jehoiachin? (2 Kin. 24:8–12; 2 Chr. 36:9, 10)

How did Nebuchadnezzar punish the kingdom of Judah for making him come against it a second time? (2 Kin. 24:13–16)

BEHIND THE SCENES

Jehoiachin's personal name before he became king was Jeconiah or the shorter Coniah. He was not eight years old (2 Chr. 36:8) because five of his seven sons (1 Chr. 3:17) were listed on a Babylonian ration document from 592 B.C.[1]

The second Babylonian attack on Jerusalem occurred in 597 B.C. The prophet Ezekiel was among the many who were deported from Jerusalem to Babylon at this time. Interestingly, the Jews in Babylon and the Jews in Jerusalem continued to think of Jehoiachin as the rightful king in exile. They dated events in terms of his reign long after he was in exile (2 Kin. 25:27; Ezek. 1:2).[2]

FAITH ALIVE

What happens in our hearts and lives when we become puppets of the world rather than servants of the Lord?

What names does the world prefer to attach to believers in the Lord Jesus to make us sound less distinctive, more like everybody else?

Who has had a ministry to you like the one of the prophet Jeremiah to these last kings of Judah—a ministry calling for spiritual separation from the world? How valuable has this witness been to you?

CAST FROM GOD'S PRESENCE

Godly King Josiah had three sons on the throne of Judah after him, but all three were wicked monarchs. The third of Josiah's sons was Mattaniah—renamed Zedekiah by his Babylonian masters (2 Kin. 24:17). Zedekiah was Jehoahaz's baby brother (compare 23:31 and 24:18). King Zedekiah presided over the last days of Judah's existence before the Babylonians got fed up with rebellion and did away with the tiny kingdom centered in Jerusalem.

What factors in the policies of Zedekiah and the life of the nation doomed Judah during this time? (2 Kin. 24:19, 20; 2 Chr. 36:12–14)

WORD WEALTH

Turning to (2 Chr. 36:13) translates a Hebrew verb that appears more than a thousand times in the Old Testament. Its primary sense is to go back to a point of departure (Ex. 4:19). In a spiritual sense it can mean either to "turn away" from God (Num. 14:43) or to "repent," to turn away from one's sin and toward God (Hos. 3:5).[3]

How did the Babylonian attack on Jerusalem unfold? (2 Kin. 25:1–3)

What happened to the army and the royal family when the Babylonians finally breached the northern wall of Jerusalem? (2 Kin. 25:4–7)

How did the Babylonian emperor Nebuchadnezzar deal with each of these after his army broke through the walls of Jerusalem?

- The structures of the city (2 Kin. 25:8–10)

- The people of the city and nation (2 Kin. 25:11, 12)

- The valuable metals in the temple furnishings (2 Kin. 25:13–17)

- The leading men of Jerusalem (2 Kin. 25:18–21)

How did the chronicler relate the fall of Jerusalem to the spiritual life of Judah and her kings throughout the period of the monarchy? (2 Chr. 36:15, 16)

FAITH ALIVE

What is the difference between the judgment of Judah at the fall of Jerusalem and the chastening the Lord brings into our lives to correct us?

How can we avoid being weak people like King Zedekiah, swayed by the opinions of others and fearful to take a stand for the Lord and His Word?

What does the fall of Judah and Jerusalem teach us about the dangers of persistent, selfish sinning paired with indifference to the correctives God sends us?

TURMOIL AND HOPE

Neither 2 Kings nor 2 Chronicles ends with its account of the fall of Jerusalem. Both hint at spiritual hope in the future. Second Kings must give a small hint, since it was written before the captivity ended. Second Chronicles gives a much larger hint, since its purpose was to renew the hope and dedication of those who were rebuilding Judah and Jerusalem after the captivity.

How did the Babylonians expect to maintain order in Judah among the peasantry left in the land to prevent the province from reverting to wilderness? (2 Kin. 25:22)

How did Gedaliah the governor pacify the survivors of the devastation caused by the Babylonian conquest? (2 Kin. 25:23, 24)

What was the outcome of Gedaliah's efforts to govern Judah on behalf of the Babylonian conquerors? (2 Kin. 25:25, 26)

BIBLE EXTRA

The Book of Jeremiah gives a great deal of detail concerning the final moments of Judah, since the prophet was God's chief spokesman on the scene to guide the kings and the people. Once Jeremiah's friend and protector Gedaliah had been assassinated by Ishmael, how did the Lord offer divine guidance to the survivors? (Jer. 42)

How did the survivors respond to the prophetic word of the Lord? (Jer. 43:1–7)

How did the chronicler explain the seventy-year length of the Babylonian exile Judah faced? (2 Chr. 36:20, 21; see Lev. 25:1–4; 26:32–35; Jer. 25:9–12)

What happened to deposed and imprisoned King Jehoiachin about halfway through the captivity that hinted of God's future blessing on a remnant of His covenant people? (2 Kin. 25:27–30)

Jerusalem was devastated by the armies of Nebuchadnezzar in 586 B.C. Babylon in turn was destroyed by the Medes and Persians under Cyrus the Great in 538 B.C. What was the policy of the first Persian emperor toward the captive people of God? (2 Chr. 36:20, 22, 23)

GOD'S KINGDOM IN MY LIFE

The whole ministry of Jesus' own preaching, teaching, and ministry centered in these words: "The kingdom of God is at hand" (Mark 1:15). He came as the Savior-Lamb to rescue and redeem mankind to know its original estate in the divine order. The dynamic of Christian life and ministry is not found in "eating and drinking" (that is, in ritual performance), but in "righteousness and peace and joy in the Holy Spirit" (Rom. 14:17).[4]

The kings of Israel and Judah were supposed to represent the Lord, who was the true Sovereign of His people. Why do you think so many of them confused their spiritual responsibility with the external rituals of monarchy?

The entire ministry of Jesus must be understood in relation to His declaration of the presence of the kingdom of God. His ethical teachings, for example, cannot be understood apart from the announcement of the kingdom. They are ethics of the kingdom; the perfection to which they point makes no sense apart from the present experience of the kingdom. Participation in the new reality of the kingdom involves a follower of Jesus in a call to the highest righteousness (Matt. 5:20).

The acts and deeds of Jesus likewise make sense only in the larger context of proclaiming the kingdom. His healings were manifestations of the presence of the kingdom. In these deeds was a direct confrontation between God and the forces of evil, or Satan and his demons (Luke 10:18). Satan and evil are in retreat now that the kingdom has entered human history (1 John 2:17). We live in anticipation of the final age of perfection that will be realized at Christ's return.[5]

All the kings of Israel and too many of the kings of Judah were on the wrong side of the confrontation between God and the powers of darkness. What impact did that have on the character and fate of those kingdoms?

Fundamental to New Testament truth is that the kingdom of God is the spiritual reality and dynamic available to each person who receives Jesus Christ as Savior and Lord. To receive Him—the King—is to receive His kingly rule, not only *in* your life and *over* your affairs, but *through* your life and *by* your service and love. "The kingdom of God is within you," Jesus said (Luke 17:21).[6]

Which attitudes and actions common to your life are incompatible with the glorious truth that the kingdom of God is within you? What attitudes and actions would you like to see replace these?

As Jesus presented post-resurrection teaching "pertaining to the kingdom of God" (Acts 1:3), He made three points. (1) The Holy Spirit is the Person and the power by which assistance and ability are given for serving others and for sharing with others the life and power of God's kingdom. (2) The Holy Spirit's power must be "received" (v. 8); it is not an automatic experience. As surely as the Holy Spirit indwells each believer (Rom. 8:9), so surely He will fill and overflow (John 7:37–39) each who receives the Holy Spirit in childlike faith. (3) When the Holy Spirit fills you, you will know it. Jesus said it and the disciples found it true (Acts 1:5; 2:1–4).[7]

As you assess the role of the Holy Spirit in God's kingdom rule of your life, what spiritual gifts has He given you? How are you opening your heart and life to the filling work of the Spirit?

We are to *welcome* the kingdom and administer situations on earth by inviting the overarching might of God's Spirit to move into difficult or impossible circumstances and transform them. This is done by praise: "In everything give thanks, for this is the will of God in Christ Jesus for you" (1 Thess. 5:18). We welcome the overruling power of God into any situation by praying "Your kingdom come, Your will be done—here." Then set up a place for God's throne by filling your life's settings with praise.[8]

What are the circumstances of your life that seem impossible? How can you pray for God's kingdom power to invade these areas? How can you prepare a place for God's throne through praise?

1. J. Barton Payne, "1, 2 Chronicles," *The Expositor's Bible Commentary*, Vol. 4 (Grand Rapids: Zondervan Publishing House, 1988), 339.

2. Donald J. Wiseman, *1 and 2 Kings: An Introduction and Commentary* (Leicester, England: InterVarsity Press, 1993), 317.

3. *Spirit-Filled Life® Bible* (Nashville: Thomas Nelson Publishers, 1991), 393, "Word Wealth, Ruth 4:15, restorer."

4. *Hayford's Bible Handbook* (Nashville: Thomas Nelson Publishers, 1995), 668, "The Kingdom of God."

5. Ibid., 667, "Kingdom of God, Kingdom of Heaven."

6. Ibid., 672, "The Kingdom of God."

7. Ibid., 674.

8. Ibid., 676.

SPIRIT-FILLED LIFE® BIBLE DISCOVERY GUIDE SERIES

*Coming Soon

SPIRIT-FILLED LIFE® KINGDOM DYNAMICS STUDY GUIDES

K 1   People of the Spirit: Gifts, Fruit, and Fullness of the
       Holy Spirit 0-8407-8431-7
K 2   Kingdom Warfare: Prayer, Spiritual Warfare, and the
       Ministry of Angels 0-8407-8433-3
K 3   God's Way to Wholeness: Divine Healing by the Power
       of the Holy Spirit 0-8407-8430-9
K 4   Life in the Kingdom: Foundations of the Faith
       0-8407-8432-5
K 5   Focusing on the Future: Key Prophecies and Practical
       Living 0-8407-8517-8
K 6   Toward More Glorious Praise: Power Principles for
       Faith-Filled People 0-8407-8518-6
K 7   Bible Ministries for Women: God's Daughters and
       God's Work 0-8407-8519-4
K 8   People of the Covenant: God's New Covenant for
       Today 0-8407-8520-8
K 9   Answering the Call to Evangelism: Spreading the Good
       News to Everyone 0-8407-2096-3
K10   Spirit-Filled Family: Holy Wisdom to Build Happy
       Homes 0-8407-2085-8
K11   Appointed to Leadership: God's Principles for Spiritual
       Leaders 0-8407-2083-1
K12   Power Faith: Balancing Faith in Words and Work
       0-8407-2094-7
K13   Race & Reconciliation: Healing the Wounds, Winning
       the Harvest 0-7852-1131-4
K14   Praying in the Spirit: Heavenly Resources for Praise and
       Intercession 0-7852-1141-1

OTHER SPIRIT-FILLED LIFE® STUDY RESOURCES

Spirit-Filled Life® Bible, available in several bindings and
       in NKJV and KJV.
Spirit-Filled Life® Bible for Students
Hayford's Bible Handbook 0-8407-8359-0